THE
PRIVATE EYE
SCHOOL

More One-Hour Mysteries for the Classroom

Mary Ann Carr

First published in 2008 by Prufrock Press Inc.

Published in 2021 by Routledge
605 Third Avenue, New York, NY 10017
2 Park Square, Milton Park, Abingdon, Oxon OX14 4RN

Routledge is an imprint of the Taylor & Francis Group, an informa business

Copyright © 2008 by Taylor & Francis Group

Production Design by Marjorie Parker
Illustrated by David Parker

ISBN: 9781032141664 (hbk)
ISBN: 9781593632946 (pbk)

DOI: 10.4324/9781003238874

CONTENTS

DEDICATION

This book is dedicated to student detectives at The College of William & Mary's Summer Enrichment Program in Williamsburg, VA.

ACKNOWLEDGEMENTS

Thank you to the following people for their invaluable help: Lausanne Davis Carpenter, set designer at Virginia Premiere Theatre in Williamsburg, VA, who inspired the mystery, *Stealing the Spotlight*. Todd Cooke, lighting designer at Virginia Premiere Theatre in Williamsburg, VA, who provided technical assistance in developing the crime scene for the *Stealing the Spotlight* mystery. Marjorie E. Harris, forensic scientist supervisor of the Bloodstain Section in the Department of Forensic Science, VA, who supplied information about bloodstain analysis which enabled me to create the forensic activities for the *Stealing the Spotlight* mystery. Don W. Strack, a collector of American Flyer trains, who provided information about vintage circus trains that led to development of *The Great Electric Train Robbery* mystery. And Gretchen Sparling, my editor at Prufrock Press, who contributed editorial input that strengthened the book.

INTRODUCTION

The Mysteries

In *The Private Eye School: More One-Hour Mysteries for the Classroom*, student detectives will utilize their investigative skills to solve this collection of unusual crimes that includes robberies, pranks, and a mystery with a red-herring twist. These mysteries require students to solve logic puzzles to determine suspects' motives and alibis. Students also will break a secret code, analyze soil and bloodstains, and compare lip prints and DNA in a forensic lab setting that you can set up in your classroom. After the closing of these mysteries, students will be eager to solve new cases, perhaps those found in the companion books, *One-Hour Mysteries* and *More One-Hour Mysteries*.

Each of the mysteries requires students to think outside of the box, organize data, take notes, make inferences, and use deductive reasoning skills. All of the mysteries include a teacher's guide and introduction, as well as attractive reproducible pages for students that provide the clues and data they will need to solve each crime. In addition to the five one-hour mysteries included in *The Private Eye School*, this book includes a set of concluding activities that will challenge students and utilize the skills this book is designed to develop. The book is composed of the following:

- *The Private Eye School and an introduction to the Robbery at the Groaning Board Restaurant*: Students will develop their sleuthing skills after completing these mini-courses designed for those who are new to the *One-Hour Mystery* series. (If your students are veteran One-Hour detectives, you may opt to skip this introductory section.) The Private Eye School section will introduce students to the skills necessary for solving crimes with activities that make students think outside the box, be a keen observer, learn detective vocabulary, ask good questions, learn new vocabulary, and make inferences and deductions. After these activities, students will be prepared to solve their first mystery, the Robbery at the Groaning Board Restaurant. This chapter will walk students through the beginning of the mystery by aiding the creation of their first suspect list.

- *The Robbery at the Groaning Board Restaurant*: The introduction to this mystery is presented in the previous section during the Private Eye School courses that introduce new detectives to the crime-solving process. In this chapter, students will go on to find the culprit of this robbery by using logic puzzles and deductive reasoning.

- *The Great Electric Train Robbery*: This mystery, designed to be a group or individual activity, requires student detectives to gather evidence by solving eight matrix logic puzzles that lead them to new clues. Students will use newspaper articles, e-mail messages, and trace evidence to solve the logic puzzles and eliminate suspects. Students also may complete a supplementary activity, during which they will act as forensic artists and sketch the suspects in a drawn-to-scale police lineup.

- *The Pizza Delivery Joke Mystery:* Love a good pizza? You wouldn't like the one delivered to the victim in this mystery. Detectives will enjoy investigating these high school suspects to determine who put worms in the pizza. They not only will establish motive and opportunity, students also will act like forensics scientists by analyzing soil and decoding a secret message.

- *Stealing the Spotlight:* Detectives will step backstage to examine the crime scene in this theatre mystery. During their investigation, they will interrogate the cast and crew of a theatrical production, eliminate suspects with logic puzzles, reconstruct the crime, and analyze bloodstains. Students will enjoy the challenge of figuring this one out with the help of DNA testing, an activity that will expose students to the real world of crime solving.

- *The Vandal Strikes:* A professional football helmet, a middle school raffle, and revenge play key roles in this red-herring mystery. Detectives will analyze a lip print and pieces of leaves found at the crime scene, only to discover that the evidence leads to a dead end. Who, then, is guilty?

- *Mystery Learning Center:* This final chapter will challenge students to create their own mystery, which includes developing a plot, characters, and logic puzzles. Students may choose to work as groups, or as individuals. After the mysteries are completed, students should swap mysteries with a classmate, or another group, and solve a different self-written crime.

How to Use This Book

Teachers or parents can use this book in a variety of ways. *The Private Eye School* is an introduction to crime solving that can be used as the activities in a thematic unit. This book also can continue your classroom's crime solving after using the companion books, *One-Hour Mysteries* and *More One-Hour Mysteries*. Another idea may be to host a "Mystery Day" once every six weeks, during which your students solve a single crime, or several crimes, from *The Private Eye School*. Each mystery requires between 1–3 hours, depending on the lab analysis, length of discussions, and student involvement.

Grade Levels

The mysteries in *The Private Eye School* were developed for students in grades 4–8. They are appropriate to be used in classes for gifted students, as well as in regular classrooms.

Skills and Standards

In addition to motivating your students, the mysteries in this book reinforce a variety of thinking skills, and address national standards in both language arts and science. In solving these mysteries, students will:

Language Arts

- Identify questions to be answered in order to solve each mystery,
- Distinguish between fact and opinion,
- Compare and contrast various viewpoints,
- Summarize information,
- Make predictions based on evidence,
- Draw conclusions and support the conclusions with evidence,
- Make inferences based on both explicit and implied information,
- Skim materials to locate specific information relating to each case,
- Differentiate between relevant and irrelevant information,
- Develop notes that include important details related to each mystery, and
- Evaluate sources.

Scientific Investigation, Reasoning, and Logic

- Apply the scientific method of investigation as it applies to forensic science,
- Collect and interpret data,
- Make observations,
- Make predictions based on patterns and/or data,
- Draw conclusions based on evidence,
- Recognize the importance of mathematics in scientific investigations, and
- Use deductive reasoning to solve matrix logic puzzles.

Happy sleuthing!

THE PRIVATE EYE SCHOOL
AND AN INTRODUCTION TO THE ROBBERY AT THE GROANING BOARD RESTAURANT

TEACHER'S GUIDE: THE PRIVATE EYE SCHOOL

Introduction

Welcome students to The Private Eye School. Explain to them that at this school, they will master skills used by real-life detectives to solve crimes. Some of these skills include: thinking outside the box, being a keen observer, learning detective vocabulary, asking good questions, making inferences, and making deductions. Use these introductory activities, or courses, to prepare students for the mysteries they will be solving later in this book as a graduate of The Private Eye School.

Courses in the Private Eye School

Thinking Outside the Box

Tell students that a great detective has to think outside of the box. Put nine dots on the board like this:

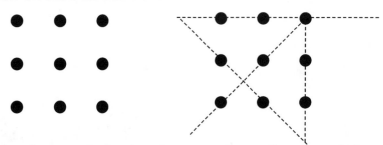

Ask students to draw nine dots on a sheet of paper and then connect all the dots using four straight lines—without lifting their pencil from the paper. After they have made several attempts, discuss how it is essential to think outside of the box when completing this task. Explain that in order to connect all of the dots without lifting the pencil, it is necessary to go beyond the boundaries set by the nine dots. Otherwise, it is impossible. The drawing to the right is the correct example of how students should connect the dots.

Becoming a Keen Observer

Select a student to stand in front of the class. Ask the class to visually study the student for 30 seconds. Then, ask the student to step out of the room. Now, ask the class to answer these questions regarding the student.

- Was he or she wearing socks?
- Was he or she wearing a watch?
- What color were his or her pants or skirt?
- What color were his or her shoes?
- How many pieces of jewelry was he or she wearing (if any)?

Bring the student back into the room and check the class' answers. Do this several times, asking a different student to stand in front of the class each time. Ask the class if they are becoming more proficient each time they do this exercise.

Learning Detective Vocabulary

Assign individual words to students in groups or by themselves, and instruct students to define the vocabulary terms. Not only must they define the term, they also should write a sentence that uses their vocabulary word, make a web with this word as a subtopic, and draw a symbol that illustrates the meaning of their word. Go over the definitions of these words as a class after students have completed the activities.

Word list:
- accomplice,
- alibi,
- cheiloscopy,
- chromatography,
- clues,
- counterfeit,
- crime,
- crime scene,
- detective,
- evidence,
- forensics,
- fingerprints,
- forgery,
- motive,
- substantiate,
- suspect, and
- trace evidence.

Asking Good Questions

Explain to students that detectives must learn to ask good questions because good questions will uncover clues that will lead to the solving of a crime. Have them discuss this statement: *Smart questions lead to smart answers.* Ask students this: What kind of questions do detectives always ask about a crime? They should come up with the answers: Who, what, when, where, why, and how. List these words in writing, such as on the chalkboard, so they are visible to your students.

Hand out The Case of the Missing Van Gogh (p. 14) and read the mystery out loud with your students. Then, discuss these six important questions regarding the mystery: Who was robbed? What was stolen? Where did the robbery take place? When did it take place? How did the culprit enter the house? Why did the robbery take place, or what's the motive?

Making Inferences

Ask students to define the word *inference*. They should answer: an inference is the act of deriving a conclusion based solely on what you already know. Explain to students that detectives use inferences about motives, timing, method of entry into a crime scene, and many other details of a crime. The detectives may use these inferences to narrow down a possible suspect list, or even while they are interrogating a suspect. However, detectives don't just jump to their own conclusions about the facts of a crime. Detectives always use evidence to support an inference that they may have about a suspect or a crime.

Provide students with the handout the Groaning Board Restaurant Crime Scene Photo (p. 15). Ask them to examine it carefully and make their own inferences about the robbery that has taken place. Have students discuss the following questions in small groups or as a group, and require students to support their inferences with factual evidence in the crime scene photo. You also may wish to require students to take notes on the answers to these questions.

- What happened? What evidence can you find in the photo that supports your answer?
- What was most likely taken? What evidence can you find to support your idea?
- Where did this happen? How do you know? What do you know about this place of business from the evidence in the photo?
- How did it happen? How did the culprit enter the building? How did the culprit open the safe and the smaller metal box? What evidence supports your idea?
- Where do you think the keys to the metal box were kept? What evidence supports your idea?
- What does the note left behind suggest about the culprit? What does this suggest about the motive for the robbery?
- What does the phone and the money on the floor suggest about the culprit?
- Who might be logical suspects in the robbery?

Ask students to discuss what observations are *relevant* to these questions and what observations are not. Using the clues in the Crime Scene Photo, what inferences can students make about the robbery? Guide students to understand that the clues in the photo suggest that the culprit is probably someone who is familiar with the restaurant and who knew that the manager would be depositing the weekly earnings the next day because the manager makes deposits on the same day every week.

Instruct students to read the handout The Robbery at the Groaning Board Restaurant (p. 16). If this is the first mystery your students have attempted, you may choose to read this handout out loud as a class. After you're done reading the mystery, it's time to introduce students to matrix logic puzzles so that they can begin determining a list of suspects.

Making Deductions

Explain to students that real-life detectives make deductions when solving crimes. Ask students to define the word *deduction* (in reference to detective work). They should respond: deductive reasoning means going from the general to the specific by using the process of elimination. In the case of a mystery, suspects are eliminated from a suspect list one by one until the culprit is identified.

Tell students that they are going to learn how to work a type of puzzle that will train them to think deductively like a detective. In these puzzles, students will fit clues together in order to find the solution. These puzzles are called *matrix logic puzzles*. Students will solve four of these puzzles as they attempt to complete The Robbery at the Groaning Board Restaurant Mystery. Some students already may be familiar with this type of puzzle. For those who are not, the puzzles in this beginners' mystery will help students learn to make deductions using logical reasoning.

THE CASE OF THE MISSING VAN GOGH

Imogene Seewell was an heiress to a vast fortune. Although she was almost deaf, her eyes were like a hawk. Everyone said that is why she spent most of her money on famous paintings. She had recently purchased an original oil painting by Vincent Van Gogh, which she hung in a gallery in her mansion on Turtle Creek Parkway.

Last Tuesday, Miss Seewell woke up at 6 a.m. as usual. She dressed and went downstairs to the gallery where she planned to have her morning coffee. After pouring herself a cup, she sank down onto the sofa. "Oh no!" she screamed, dropping her cup onto the floor. "It can't be!" She pointed toward the blank wall where her newest painting had been. "My Van Gogh. It's gone!"

She immediately called the police. "Someone has stolen my favorite Van Gogh!" she exclaimed. "It's worth millions. I must get it back!"

Detectives asked Miss Seewell if she had recently told anyone about the Van Gogh. "Only my cousin, Arthur Seewell," she said. "He has always loved my art. And, he's always been angry that I have it and he doesn't. He has told me more times than I can count that he should have inherited our grandfather's money and not me."

Miss Seewell shook her head. "I should have suspected something was amiss yesterday," she said. "He came to see me and suggested that I give him a key to my house so he could get in if something happened and I became ill. I thought at the time it was a good idea. I'm quite an old lady, you know. So, I gave him the key."

Detectives searched the gallery, the house, and the garden outside the gallery window, searching for clues. They found no sign of forced entry. And, they found no clues.

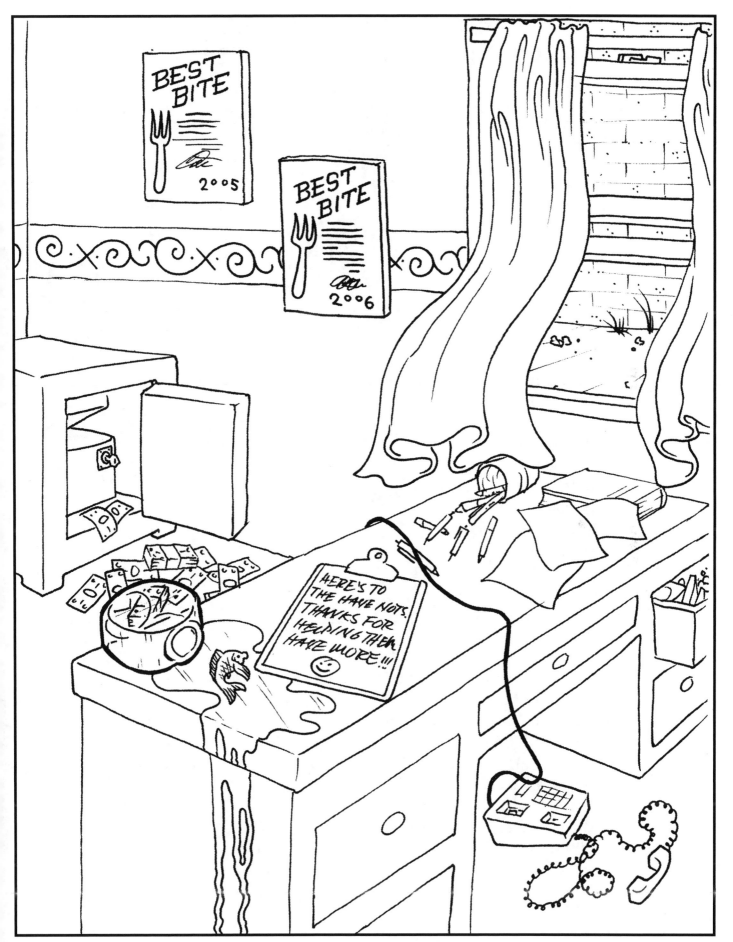

THE ROBBERY AT THE GROANING BOARD RESTAURANT

The Groaning Board Restaurant is an upscale, downtown eatery, owned and operated by Leo Rainwater. The food and atmosphere at The Groaning Board has a very good reputation in the downtown area of Center City.

This Friday morning was like every morning to Mr. Rainwater, who got up around 9 a.m. after spending a late night at the restaurant. He dressed and ate a late breakfast, preparing himself for another long, yet profitable day.

When Mr. Rainwater arrived at the restaurant, he grabbed a cup of coffee and walked back to his office to take care of some business matters,

including a trip to the bank to deposit the weekly earnings.

After entering his office, Mr. Rainwater noticed that the door to his safe was open, and that the metal box inside was empty—the $10,000 in cash he had left in the box the night before was gone!

He rushed to his desk to call the police, but his phone was knocked off the desk and lying on the floor. His desk was a mess, and lying on his clipboard was a message: "Here's to the have nots! Thanks for helping them have more!"

Mr. Rainwater was outraged, and phoned the police. Now, it's your job to assist the detectives in finding the theft who stole from the Groaning Board Restaurant!

THE ROBBERY
AT THE GROANING BOARD
RESTAURANT

TEACHER'S GUIDE: THE ROBBERY AT THE GROANING BOARD RESTAURANT

Introduction

Now that students have sharpened their sleuthing skills, they will be ready to solve their first mystery in *The Private Eye School*. If you skipped the previous introductory chapter, you will need to hand out copies of The Groaning Board Restaurant Crime Scene Photo (p. 15) and The Robbery at the Groaning Board Restaurant (p. 16). You may choose to read the mystery aloud to your students, or (if you have already read the story as instructed in the introduction chapter) re-read the mystery so that students may take notes.

Now, you will instruct students to solve The Robbery at the Groaning Board Restaurant. While you are guiding students through the logic puzzles, remember that all of the answers to the puzzles can be found at the end of the Teacher's Guide (pp. 19–20).

Solving the Mystery

Hand out copies of Detective Notes (p. 21) to students and allow them to read the notes, discuss amongst themselves, and take their own notes. Explain to students that the detectives' notes helped determine a suspect list. Now that they have a list of suspects, detectives need to gather information about each of the suspects. This is how your students will be assisting the detectives. Explain to students that they will uncover more facts about the suspects by solving matrix logic puzzles and making deductions.

Hand out copies of the Employees at the Groaning Board Restaurant puzzle (p. 22). Ask students to complete the matrix logic puzzle to determine the position of each employee and his or her length of employment at the restaurant. If your students are new to logic puzzles, you may wish to allow them to work in small groups to solve the first puzzle.

Tell students that the chief detective on this case interviewed five witnesses. Each witness said that they saw a person crawling out of the window of Leo Rainwater's office yesterday evening around 11:30 p.m. Each witness also said that they noticed something specific about the culprit—but all of the details were different. Hand out copies of the Five Witnesses handouts (pp. 23–24) to students and direct them to complete the puzzle and determine what each witness said that they noticed about the person crawling out of the office window. Discuss the evidence that students believe points to the culprit. Students should deduct from the puzzle that the culprit has dark hair and is wearing blue jeans and sneakers.

Hand out Who Is the Culprit? puzzles (pp. 25–26) and direct students to complete the remaining two puzzles to determine which suspect is guilty based on the evidence provided by the five witnesses. You may want to involve students in a group discussion to review their final solution to the crime. Use the Conclusion and Answer Key below to check your students' understanding.

Conclusion

Read the following conclusion to your students:

When the evidence was presented to Mr. Grow, he hung his head and admitted that he was guilty. "I'm so sorry," he said. "I was angry because I heard Mr. Rainwater say to the chef that he was unhappy with my recipes and was thinking about firing me and promoting the other chef to my position." Mr. Grow admitted that it was wrong to steal and he gave the money back to Mr. Rainwater, promising never to steal again. He also promised Mr. Rainwater that if he would give him another chance, he would learn new recipes and would never serve liver and onions again.

After reading the conclusion, congratulate students on solving their first mystery. Discuss any discrepancies your students may have experienced when eliminating suspects with the logic puzzles. You may also wish to discuss the skills that were required of your students when solving this crime, such as deductive reasoning, thinking outside of the box, asking good questions, and so forth. Now that your students have solved their first mystery, they will be eager to move on to the next crime in *The Private Eye School*, The Great Electric Train Robbery (p. 27).

Answer Key

Employees at the Groaning Board Restaurant Puzzle

Mrs. Blake, hostess, 6 years; Ms. Still, chef, 2 ½ years; Ms. Keene, waitress, 2 years; Mr. Grow, head chef, 4 years; Mr. Dunn, waiter, 1 year.

Five Witnesses Puzzle

Jones, office window, jeans; Weaver, bus, tripped; Cross, apartment window, sneakers; Stone, car, carrying a bag; Wood, Harley, brown hair.

Who Is the Culprit? Puzzle 1

Mrs. Blake, black hair; Ms. Still, grey hair; Ms. Keene, blonde hair; Mr. Grow, brown hair; Mr. Dunn is bald.

Who Is the Culprit? Puzzle 2

Mrs. Blake, brown pants, clogs; Ms. Still, tan pants, Jet Speed sneakers; Ms. Keene, white pants, high heels; Mr. Grow, blue jeans, Lightning sneakers; Mr. Dunn, black pants, boots. *The two puzzles reveal that Mr. Grow was the culprit.*

DETECTIVE NOTES

After interviewing Leo Rainwater, manager of the Groaning Board Restaurant, detectives took the following notes pertaining to the case. Read them carefully. Do any of these facts provide evidence to support the inferences you made about the crime after examining the crime scene?

1. The Groaning Board Restaurant is an expensive restaurant that has a reputation for its delicious food.
2. The restaurant earns thousands of dollars each week.
3. Mr. Rainwater keeps all of the weekly cash earnings in a safe in his office and deposits them in the bank every Friday afternoon.
4. Last Friday morning, Mr. Rainwater arrived at the restaurant and saw that the door to his office safe was wide open, and that the metal cash box inside was empty.
5. $10,000 was in a metal lock box in the safe.
6. A stack of $20 bills was found lying on the floor in front of the safe.
7. The lock to the box and its key were found on the floor beside the stack of bills.
8. A handwritten note that read, "Here's to the have nots! Thanks for helping them have more!," was found attached to a clipboard on his desk.
9. After the restaurant closed Thursday evening, Mr. Rainwater said that he added the day's cash earnings to the other money in the safe. He said he then locked both the metal box and the door to the safe.
10. He said he put the slip of paper with the safe's combination and the key to the lock box in his desk drawer.
11. Mr. Rainwater said that he left the restaurant Thursday at 10:00 P.M. and returned Friday morning at 10:30 A.M.
12. The restaurant has five employees.
13. According to Mr. Rainwater, all of the employees know that Mr. Rainwater deposits the cash earnings every Friday afternoon.
14. Also, all of the employees at one time or another have been in his office when Mr. Rainwater opened both the safe and the metal lock box.

EMPLOYEES AT THE GROANING BOARD RESTAURANT

Detectives questioned the employees at the Groaning Board Restaurant after the robbery was discovered. In addition to Leo Rainwater, the restaurant manager, there are five employees: Mrs. Blake, Ms. Still, Ms. Keene, Mr. Grow, and Mr. Dunn. They hold the following positions: waitress, waiter, head chef, chef, and hostess.

Read the clues to determine what position each person held and how long he or she has worked at the restaurant. Hint: You must consider gender when solving this puzzle (the male waiter and female waitress).

Employees	Positions					# of Years at Restaurant				
	Waitress	Waiter	Head Chef	Chef	Hostess	1	2	2½	4	6
Mrs. Blake										
Ms. Still										
Ms. Keene										
Mr. Grow										
Mr. Dunn										
1										
2										
2½										
4										
6										

Clues:
1. Mrs. Blake has worked at the restaurant for 6 years.
2. The head chef has worked at the restaurant longer than the chef but not as long as the hostess.
3. Ms. Still has worked ½ year longer than the waitress.
4. The waiter, Mr. Dunn, was hired most recently.

FIVE WITNESSES

The chief detective on this case interviewed five witnesses. Each witness said that they saw a person crawling out of the window of Leo Rainwater's office yesterday evening around 11:30 p.m.

The Groaning Board Restaurant is on a corner of the downtown district of a large city. When the witnesses saw the culprit, three of them said that they were stopped in their vehicles at an intersection while waiting for the light to turn green. One witness said that they saw the culprit while looking out his home window in the apartment above the restaurant. Another witness said that she saw the culprit from her office window across the street from the restaurant.

Each witness told the detective a specific detail that he or she remembered about the culprit, such as his or her clothing or appearance, but all five of the witnesses remembered seeing different things. One noticed that the culprit had brown hair. Another noticed that the culprit was wearing blue jeans. Still another noticed that the culprit was wearing sneakers. Another said the culprit was carrying a bag, and another claimed the culprit tripped when running away from the restaurant.

Read the clues to determine what each witness was doing and what he or she noticed about the culprit.

FIVE WITNESSES

Witnesses	What Each Witness Was Doing					What Each Witness Noticed				
	Riding a bus	Riding in a car	Riding on a Harley	Looking out of an apartment window	Looking out of an office window	Brown hair	Jeans	Sneakers	Carrying a bag	Tripped
Jones										
Weaver										
Cross										
Stone										
Wood										
Brown Hair										
Jeans										
Sneakers										
Carrying a Bag										
Tripped										

Clues:

1. Jones and another witness (who said that he noticed the culprit's sneakers) were looking out of a window in a building. Hint: This means that Jones can't be the one who said the culprit was wearing sneakers.
2. Stone and the witness on the bus were both riding home from work.
3. The witness who noticed the bag was in a car.
4. Wood was on his brand-new Harley.
5. Weaver saw the culprit trip.
6. The witness who noticed the culprit was wearing jeans was working late in his office.

WHO IS THE CULPRIT?

After reviewing the detective's interview with each of the witnesses, you reviewed your detective notes to determine if any of the suspects fit the description of the person seen climbing out of Rainwater's office window. Solve these two matrix logic puzzles below to find out which suspect, if any, has dark hair and was wearing both sneakers and blue jeans.

First, read the clues to determine what color hair each suspect had.

Suspects	Color of Hair				
	black	bald	gray	blonde	brown
Mrs. Blake					
Ms. Still					
Ms. Keene					
Mr. Grow					
Mr. Dunn					

Clues:

1. Mr. Grow and the bald-headed man are friends.
2. Ms. Keene loves her blonde hair.
3. Mrs. Blake and the man with brown hair are the only two suspects with dark hair.

WHO IS THE CULPRIT?

Next, read the clues below to determine what color of pants and type of shoes each suspect was wearing the day of the crime.

Names	Color of Pants					Type of Shoes				
	Brown pants	Tan pants	Blue jeans	Black pants	White jeans	Clogs	High Heels	Boots	Jet Speed Sneakers	Lightning Sneakers
Mrs. Blake										
Ms. Still										
Ms. Keene										
Mr. Grow										
Mr. Dunn										
Clogs										
High Heels										
Boots										
Jet Speed Sneakers										
Lightning Sneakers										

Clues:
1. The suspect in tan pants was wearing Jet Speed sneakers, while the suspect in Lightning sneakers was wearing blue jeans.
2. Mr. Grow and the man in boots were wearing dark pants.
3. Ms. Still and the woman wearing brown pants are cousins.
4. Mrs. Blake's clogs were white, like Mrs. Keene's pants.

Who is the culprit? _____

THE GREAT ELECTRIC TRAIN ROBBERY

TEACHER'S GUIDE: THE GREAT ELECTRIC TRAIN ROBBERY

Introduction

The question in this mystery is "Who stole the antique toy train?" In order to identify the thief, student detectives must solve eight matrix logic puzzles. Each puzzle provides a clue relating to the suspects or to evidence found at the crime scene. The clues will enable detectives to eliminate the suspects from the suspect list, one by one, until only the culprit remains. A series of newspaper articles and e-mails also provide information relevant to the case.

Solving the Mystery

To introduce the mystery, ask students if they have ever owned an electric train. Then, hand out The Great Electric Train Robbery (p. 31). Read and discuss with your students why vintage trains are considered to be rare. Ask students why someone might want to steal this particular train set.

Hand out the newspaper articles, Extra! Extra! Read All About it! (pp. 32–33). Ask students to read the articles and then discuss if any of this information might help solve the crime. Next, hand out the first logic puzzle, Who Might Want the Train? (pp. 34–35). After students solve this puzzle, discuss which suspect might have a motive. Hand out the series of e-mails (pp. 36–37) and tell students that as they read these, they should continue thinking about motive. Discuss the questions at the bottom of the handout relating to the e-mails.

Give students the interview with Mr. Zilliman, When Did the Crime Occur? (p. 38). Read and discuss. Then, hand out the next two puzzles, Where Did You Come From? and Arrival Time in Center City (p. 39 and pp. 40–41). After students have solved these, discuss who might be eliminated from the suspect list because of this evidence.

Now, hand out the next two puzzles, Talking to Witnesses and What Were You Doing? (pp. 42–43 and p. 44). Who can be eliminated from the suspect list as a result of the evidence found in these puzzles?

Hand out Trace Evidence (pp. 45–46). Discuss this type of evidence with your students. Then, ask students to solve the last two puzzles, Trace Evidence and Another Fiber is Found (p. 47). After they have solved these and identified the culprit, read the mystery's conclusion aloud.

Supplementary Activity

Witnesses played an important role in the solving of this mystery. This supplementary activity focuses on the description of the suspects provided by witnesses. The activity requires students to think like a forensic artist and draw a picture of each suspect based on the witnesses' descriptions. Students will use the data to sketch a drawn-to-scale line-up of all of the suspects.

Hand out Forensics Artists (p. 48). Explain to students that it is important to read each description carefully, so that they can draw each detail accurately. Discuss scale drawings. Give students a sheet of graph paper and instruct them to draw a suspect lineup, using the squares on the paper as a guide.

Conclusion

When detectives presented all of the evidence to Ray Slade, he confessed. He explained that after the auction in April, he had pleaded with Mr. Zilliman to sell him the boxes that housed the train set. "When he refused, I guess I lost my temper," he said. "I desperately wanted those boxes." He explained that his father had given him a circus train set years ago when he was a small boy but he had thrown the boxes away. "Before I became a collector, I didn't realize just how valuable a train set in its original boxes could be," he said. "I'm sorry for breaking into Mr. Zilliman's house. I know it was wrong. Crime just doesn't pay. I also know that a bad temper can get a person in trouble."

Slade gave the boxes back to Mr. Zilliman who refused to press charges. "I don't think Slade is an evil man," Mr. Zilliman said. "I just think his desires got the best of him." In exchange for dropping the charges, Slade agreed to take a course in anger management and to work 300 hours in public service.

Answer Key

Who Might Want the Train? Puzzle 1

Chuck Borinski, coach; Marvin Muller, locomotive; Ray Slade, the boxes, Anna Tolbert, Pullman; and Ralph Yonkers, flat cars.

Who Might Want the Train? Puzzle 2

Glenn Cuffee, zebra and rhino; Lilly Layne, panther and pelican; Sam Newton, gorilla and pelican; Isabelle Parker, lion and panther.

Where Did You Come From?

Chuck Borinski, Chicago; Lilly Layne, Seattle; Marvin Muller, Boston; Sam Newton, Omaha; Isabelle Parker, Denver; Ray Slade, Miami; and Ralph Yonkers, Dallas.

Arrival Time in Center City

Chuck Borinski, 6:30 a.m., Speed Trip; Lilly Layne, 5:00 p.m., Top Flight; Marvin Muller, 9:00 a.m., Travel Air; Sam Newton, 1:00 p.m.,

Wing Tip; Isabelle Parker, 8:15 a.m., Wind Flow; Ray Slade, 7:30 a.m., Air Tram; Ralph Yonkers, 10:45 a.m., Jet Speed. All of the suspects arrived in Center City in time to commit the crime except for Lilly Layne who arrived at 5:00 p.m. on Top Flight. Mr. Zilliman lives 50 minutes away from the airport so it is obvious that Lilly would not have had time to reach his house and steal the train before Mr. Zilliman arrived home at 5:30.

Talking to Witnesses

Chuck Borinski, forest-green Jeep; Marvin Muller, dark-blue GMC; Sam Newton, white sports car; Isabelle Parker, brown Islander; Ray Slade, black Blazer; Ralph Yonkers, maroon Explorer. From this evidence, Sam Newton can be eliminated because he was not driving a dark-colored SUV.

What Were You Doing?

Chuck Borinski, 1:30 p.m., Gilbert exhibit; Marvin Muller, 1:45 p.m., layout exhibit; Isabelle Parker, 2:30 p.m., auction; Ray Slade, 5:00 p.m., train race; Ralph Yonkers, 1:00 p.m., workshop. Ralph Yonkers could not have been at Mr. Zilliman's house.

Trace Evidence

Chuck Borinski, white cat; Marvin Muller, brown lab; Isabelle Parker, blonde cocker; Ray Slade, black shepherd.

Another Fiber is Found

Chuck Borinski, polyester shirt; Marvin Muller, linen jacket; Isabelle Parker, silk vest; Ray Slade, cotton pants. *Ray Slade is the culprit.*

THE GREAT ELECTRIC TRAIN ROBBERY

Boys and girls love electric toy trains, and so do train collectors. In fact, a collector will spend hundreds of dollars to buy a train set if it is an antique that is in excellent condition. A vintage train is rare, and therefore very valuable. The inventor of the Erector Set, A. C. Gilbert, owned the American Flyer Company, which made many vintage trains in the 1930s, 40s, and 50s.

Antique train collectors frequently attend train meets. At these meets, collectors have the opportunity to talk with one another about their shared passion, electric toy trains. In addition, collectors can buy and sell antique trains, train tracks, and various model buildings, which they use when building train layout displays. You may recall that department stores sometimes put model train layouts in their store windows at Christmas time.

During a recent train meet in Center City, an electric train robbery occurred. Mr. Zilliman, a well-known train collector from Center City, was robbed. A thief broke into Mr. Zilliman's house while the collector was conducting a workshop at the train meet. Mr. Zilliman's prize 1950 American Flyer Circus Train set was stolen.

As detective on the case, you will need to identify the thief by solving eight matrix logic puzzles. Each puzzle provides clues that point to the culprit. In addition, you will examine other evidence: a Center City newspaper and a series of e-mails sent to Mr. Zilliman. These puzzles and evidence will help you use your deductive reasoning skills to eliminate suspects and determine the culprit. Who stole Mr. Zilliman's antique train? It's your job to find out!

EXTRA! EXTRA! READ ALL ABOUT IT!

You are the detective assigned to the case of the missing electric train. To learn more about the crime, read these newspaper articles related to this crime.

A CHAT WITH MR. ZILLIMAN

Monday, April 16

I met Mr. Zilliman in his home on Riverside Drive to talk about his favorite passion, antique trains. In addition to viewing his famous layouts complete with miniature buildings, bridges, and mountains, I was thrilled to see his latest acquisition: a 1950 American Flyer Circus Train set.

"For years, I was interested only in prewar trains, those made before 1941," Zilliman said. "Then, I spotted the circus set at an auction last weekend and that was it. I knew it had to be mine." Zilliman bid against nine other collectors. "It was tense," he said. "Those people really wanted this set but I kept bidding until it was mine. The other bidders weren't happy." Since the auction, several collectors have contacted him, asking him to sell the set. "I wouldn't think of selling it," he said.

"This set is one of the rarest collections because of its excellent condition, and also because each car comes in its original box. This makes the collection worth almost twice as much because it's very rare to find a collection with all of the original boxes."

When I asked him why he wasn't exhibiting his new circus train this year, he told me that the delay is because he's working on the elaborate circus layout that he plans to showcase at next year's train meet. "It will be my best layout yet," he said.

COME TO THE CIRCUS, THE GREATEST SHOW ON EARTH

Wednesday, April 18

The American Flyer Circus Train made by the A. C. Gilbert Company in the 1950s was the main attraction in last weekend's electric toy train auction in Center City. This train set is in perfect condition, complete with its original car boxes.

The train set features many different circus animals. Amongst these animals are panthers, zebras, rhinos, gorillas, lions, and pelicans. The train set displays two trains, each featuring a flatcar to display the various animals in cages. The variety and intricacy of the animals added tremendous interest and value to the American Flyer Circus Train collection when the auction began.

10 bidders went head-to-head, wagering hundreds of dollars in hope of owning this prestigious collection. Howard Zilliman, a well-known collector, won the auction by out-bidding the others with a final price of $1,500.

EXTRA! EXTRA! READ ALL ABOUT IT!

TRAIN MEET

Sunday, May 13

The Train Collectors Club conducted their annual train meet in Center City at the coliseum yesterday from 9 a.m. to 6:30 p.m. Visitors enjoyed several train exhibits and an auction. Howard Zilliman, a well-known collector of American Flyer trains, conducted an afternoon workshop on the topic of building miniature train layouts. A train race was the final event of the day.

VALUABLE ELECTRIC TRAIN STOLEN

Monday, May 14

A valuable American Flyer electric toy circus train was stolen Saturday from the home of Howard Zilliman, a well-known collector of vintage American Flyer trains. Zilliman had recently purchased the train at an auction. "It is a treasure," Zilliman said. "It's very valuable because it's in excellent condition. I'm heartbroken."

If anyone has information about this crime, please notify the authorities.

Based on the articles above, what information do you have about the crime that may help you solve it?

_____

_____

_____

_____

_____

_____

_____

_____

_____

_____

WHO MIGHT WANT THE TRAIN?

Based on the newspaper articles, you can deduce that the train was stolen from Mr. Zilliman's home in Center City on Saturday, May 12, the same day as the city's big train meet. You also should have noted that Mr. Zilliman was most likely at the train meet when the crime occurred. Your notes should further include that the stolen train was bought at an auction where Mr. Zilliman won a heated bidding war with a group of fellow collectors.

Nine collectors were at the recent train auction and bid against Mr. Zilliman for the circus train set. Although all of them bid on the entire set, five of them particularly wanted a specific piece of the set to add to their own collection. These pieces included the 353 locomotive and tender, the coach car, the Pullman car, the flat car, and the original boxes for the individual cars.

As the detective on the case, you believe these specific bidders may have shown motive to commit the robbery. Use the clues to find out what piece each collector wanted.

Suspects	Locomotive	Coach	Pullman	Flat Car	Boxes
Chuck Borinski					
Marvin Muller					
Ray Slade					
Anna Tolbert					
Ralph Yonkers					

Clues:

1. The man who wanted the coach had met Ralph Yonkers at last year's train meet.
2. Chuck Borinski and the man who wanted the boxes were the highest bidders next to Zilliman.
3. Ray Slade was interested in either the locomotive or the boxes.
4. Anna Tolbert and the man who wanted the flat car both have been collectors for 10 years.
5. Marvin Muller was interested in locomotives.

WHO MIGHT WANT THE TRAIN?

Four of the collectors were interested in the set because of the animals it contained. Each one wanted a particular pair of animals. Use the clues to figure out what pair each collector wanted.

	Zebra/Rhino	Lion/Panther	Gorilla/Pelican	Panther/Pelican
Glenn Cuffee				
Lilly Layne				
Sam Newton				
Isabelle Parker				

Clues:

1. Lilly Layne wanted a pelican, but didn't care about a gorilla.
2. Sam Newton and the man who wanted a zebra built a layout for their collection.
3. Isabelle Parker had every animal in her collection except for the lion.

After completing these two puzzles, what did you learn about the motive for this crime?

_____

_____

_____

_____

_____

_____

_____

Is there any suspect who has no motive?_____

PERTINENT E-MAILS SENT TO MR. ZILLIMAN

After solving the puzzles, you should have determined that all of the other bidders could be potential suspects for the theft because they wanted to own the train set (or individual pieces of the set that were up for sale). As the detective on the case, you decide to dig a little further, examining these three important e-mails found on Mr. Zilliman's computer. Remember: You are searching for a motive.

Subject: Congratulations!
From: "Glenn Cuffee" Cuff@scapenet.com
Date: 20 April 2007 08:32:01 –0400
To: "Howard Zilliman" trainman@globenet.com

Hi, old friend. Congratulations on your latest purchase. I'm so happy that you outbid Mr. Muller. I'm sure he was disgruntled that you had more money than he did. I'm sorry I'll have to miss the meet in May but I'm having surgery. I know your exhibit will be as great as usual.

Glenn

Subject: What Luck!
From: "Anna Tolbert" trainlover@ airborne.net
Date: 26 April 2007 10:46:04 –0600
To: "Howard Zilliman" trainman@ globenet.com

Dear Mr. Zilliman,

I enjoyed seeing you at the auction earlier this month. You have always helped me find trains for my collection. Thanks for the lead about another Circus Train set that is as desirable as the one I lost (because of your higher bid) at the auction. I have contacted the collector, and he is willing to sell it to me. I so appreciate your help. I'm looking forward to seeing you at the train meet in May.

Anna

Subject: Locomotive
From: "Marvin Muller" collectatrain@bayou. net
Date: 27 April 2007 12:46:00 –0200
To: "Howard Zilliman" trainman@globenet. com

Mr. Zilliman,

I can't say how disappointed I was when you kept bidding on the Circus Train at the auction. My passion is collecting great locomotives and the one on that train set is as good as new. I am genuinely upset that you wouldn't consider selling this great car to me. Please. I must have it. I'll be at the train meet and we can discuss it.

Marvin

PERTINENT E-MAILS SENT TO MR. ZILLIMAN

How are these e-mails important to this case?

_____

_____

_____

_____

_____

Can you eliminate any suspects based on the e-mails? If so, how?

_____

_____

_____

_____

_____

Can you pinpoint anyone's motive based on these e-mails? If so, how?

_____

_____

_____

_____

_____

WHEN DID THE CRIME OCCUR?

After reading the e-mails you should have eliminated Glenn Cuffee and Anna Tolbert from your list of suspects, because they are both friends with Mr. Zilliman. Anna even has another train set that she said she plans to purchase, according to her e-mail message. As the detective on the case, you next interviewed Mr. Zilliman to determine when the crime was committed. Review the facts he told you, listed below.

"I spent Saturday morning at home, going over last minute details for my workshop."

"I left home at 12:30 p.m. and arrived at the train meet at the coliseum at 1 p.m."

"My workshop began at 1:30 p.m. and lasted until 4:30. I left shortly after that, stopped at the store down the street, and got home at 5:30 p.m. I went to the room where I keep my layout and discovered that my prized train was missing."

"My workshop was advertised in both the newspaper and the train collector's newsletter so a lot of people knew that I would be gone all afternoon."

"I have been planning to get a security system on my house but just haven't done so."

"I live alone."

From this information, when do you think the crime was probably committed? Can you pinpoint a certain time frame for the crime?

_____

_____

_____

_____

_____

WHERE DID YOU COME FROM?

From Mr. Zilliman's statements, you've determined that the crime must have been committed between 12:30 and 5:30 p.m. on the Saturday of the train meet. As the detective on the case, you asked the suspects if they were in Center City that Saturday. In your investigation, you discovered that all of the suspects live out of town and flew into Center City on the day of the crime. Use the clues to find out where each suspect lives. Then, use the solution of this puzzle to help you in the following puzzle.

Suspects	Denver	Dallas	Seattle	Boston	Chicago	Miami	Omaha
Chuck Borinski							
Lilly Layne							
Marvin Muller							
Sam Newton							
Isabelle Parker							
Ray Slade							
Ralph Yonkers							

Clues:
1. Lilly and the woman from Denver had been collectors for the same number of years.
2. Chuck is from either Chicago or Miami.
3. Sam is from either Seattle or Omaha.
4. Marvin is from either Chicago or Boston.
5. Ray loves living in Florida.
6. The woman had recently moved to Seattle.

ARRIVAL TIME IN CENTER CITY

All of the suspects flew into Center City on Saturday. Read the clues to determine when they arrived and what airline they used. This information will determine whether or not the suspects had the opportunity to commit the crime. If their flight was delayed and they arrived after the time of the crime, they could not have committed it. Another important fact to know as you eliminate suspects is that it takes at least 50 minutes to drive from Mr. Zilliman's house to the airport. *Hint*: Note the intervals between the arrival times before reading the clues.

Clues:

1. The suspect who arrived an hour after Chuck Borinski was traveling on Air Tram.
2. The suspect from Denver arrived 45 minutes after Ray Slade and 45 minutes before the suspect from Boston.
3. The suspect who arrived at 1 p.m. flew Wing Tip.
4. The suspect who arrived at 9 a.m. flew Travel Air, while the suspect from Dallas flew Jet Speed.
5. The suspect traveling on Speed Trip was the first to arrive while the last to arrive flew Top Flight.
6. The suspect who lives in Seattle had a delayed flight. She didn't arrive in Center City until 5 p.m.

ARRIVAL TIME IN CENTER CITY

Suspects	6:30 a.m.	7:30 a.m.	8:15 a.m.	9:00 a.m.	10:45 a.m.	1:00 p.m.	5:00 p.m.	Travel Air	Air Tram	Top Flight	Jet Speed	Wind Flow	Wing Tip	Speed Trip
Chuck Borinski														
Lilly Layne														
Marvin Muller														
Sam Newton														
Isabelle Parker														
Ray Slade														
Ralph Yonkers														
Travel Air														
Air Tram														
Top Flight														
Jet Speed														
Wind Flow														
Wing Tip														
Speed Trip														

After completing this puzzle, what did you learn about the suspects and their opportunity to commit the crime? Can you eliminate any of the suspects?

_____

_____

_____

TALKING TO WITNESSES

The Arrival Time puzzle should eliminate Lilly Lane as a suspect, because her flight did not arrive until 5 p.m. (and she would not have had the time to drive the 50 minutes from the airport to Mr. Zilliman's house before he arrived home at 5:30 p.m.). You decide to question Mr. Zilliman's neighbor to find out if he noticed anything suspicious on the day of the crime. These are your notes from the interview:

The man next door stated that he saw a dark-colored SUV that afternoon. "It was parked in the alley right behind Mr. Zilliman's property," he said. "I had gone out back to empty my trash in the big garbage can in the alley around 4 p.m. When I opened my back gate, I saw the car speed away so fast that dirt flew up behind it. Unfortunately, I didn't get a look at the driver and I can't remember the color or make of the vehicle. I just know it was a dark-colored SUV."

After interviewing the neighbor, you will need to gather some information about who may have been driving a dark-colored SUV. You learned that six of the suspects rented a car at the airport when visiting Center City for the meet. Use the clues to find out what color and type of vehicle each one rented.

Clues:
1. Ray and the man in the maroon Explorer never rent any vehicle except SUVs.
2. Isabelle rented either the Islander or the Blazer.
3. Chuck rented a Jeep, and Ralph rented an SUV that was either maroon or blue.
4. Marvin's vehicle was a dark blue, whereas Sam's vehicle was white.
5. The Islander was brown, and the sports car was either white or black.
6. Ray's Blazer was black.

TALKING TO WITNESSES

Suspects	Explorer SUV	Jeep SUV	GMC SUV	Blazer SUV	Islander SUV	Sports Car	Brown	Black	Dark Blue	White	Forest Green	Maroon
Chuck Borinski												
Marvin Muller												
Sam Newton												
Isabelle Parker												
Ray Slade												
Ralph Yonkers												
Brown												
Black												
Dark Blue												
White												
Forest Green												
Maroon												

Why is it important to find out what type of vehicle each suspect rented? Can any suspect be eliminated as a result of this evidence?

_____

_____

_____

_____

_____

WHAT WERE YOU DOING?

Your next job as detective on this case is to question the suspects to find out where they were on Saturday after they arrived in Center City. Each suspect was seen at a variety of locations at the train meet that afternoon. Use the clues to determine where and when each suspect was seen.

Suspects	Auction	Workshop	Layout Exhibit	Gilbert Exhibit	Train Race	1:00 p.m.	1:30 p.m.	1:45 p.m.	2:30 p.m.	5:00 p.m.
Chuck Borinski										
Marvin Muller										
Isabelle Parker										
Ray Slade										
Ralph Yonkers										
1:00 p.m.										
1:30 p.m.										
1:45 p.m.										
2:30 p.m.										
5:00 p.m.										

Clues:

1. A suspect was seen arriving at the auction at 2:30 p.m. but was not seen after that.
2. The suspect who was at Mr. Zilliman's workshop arrived at 1 p.m. and stayed until 5 when he helped Mr. Zilliman load his workshop materials into his car.
3. Chuck was seen at 1:30 p.m. but at no other time during the afternoon.
4. Ray Slade was seen at the train race.
5. A suspect was seen at 1:45 p.m. at the layout exhibit.
6. Ralph and the man at the layout exhibit never went to the auction.

It takes 30 minutes to drive from the coliseum to Mr. Zilliman's house. With that knowledge after completing this puzzle, is there a suspect that you can eliminate from the list because he or she didn't have the opportunity to commit the crime?

_____

TRACE EVIDENCE

Criminals always leave something at the scene of a crime. They don't usually realize it, however, because the clue they leave behind is often invisible to the untrained eye. This tiny evidence is called *trace evidence*.

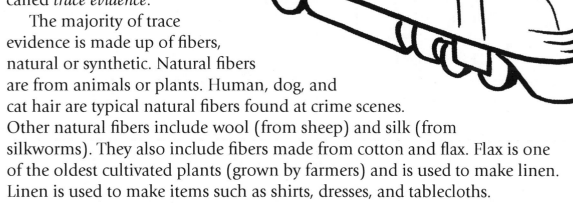

The majority of trace evidence is made up of fibers, natural or synthetic. Natural fibers are from animals or plants. Human, dog, and cat hair are typical natural fibers found at crime scenes. Other natural fibers include wool (from sheep) and silk (from silkworms). They also include fibers made from cotton and flax. Flax is one of the oldest cultivated plants (grown by farmers) and is used to make linen. Linen is used to make items such as shirts, dresses, and tablecloths.

Synthetic fibers were developed in the 1920s when rayon was first manufactured. Prior to that time, all cloth was natural. Over the next few decades, many new fibers were developed, including nylon and polyester.

The CSI team found a black fiber on Mr. Zilliman's circus layout. It could not be traced back to Mr. Zilliman. After analysis, the fiber was determined to be dog hair. As the detective on the case, you questioned the remaining suspects to find out about their pets. Use the clues to determine the color and type of pet each suspect owns.

Clues:
1. Isabelle and the man with the shepherd recently adopted their dogs from the SPCA.
2. One of the suspects has a blonde cocker or a black shepherd.
3. Marvin's chocolate lab is 12 years old.
4. Like Mr. Zilliman, Chuck is allergic to dog hair.

TRACE EVIDENCE

Suspects	Shepherd Mix	Lab Mix	Cocker Spaniel	Cat	Blonde	White	Black	Brown
Chuck Borinski								
Marvin Muller								
Isabelle Parker								
Ray Slade								
Blonde								
White								
Black								
Brown								

Why is this information important?

_____

_____

_____

_____

_____

ANOTHER FIBER IS FOUND

In addition to the dog hair, the CSI team found a white thread. It was found to be cotton, a natural fiber used in clothing. After questioning witnesses, you find that on the day of the crime all of the suspects wore some type of white clothing.

As detective on the case, you examined the clothing worn by each suspect to see if the fiber in the clothing matched that found at the crime scene. Use the clues to figure out the type of fabric and the piece of white clothing that each suspect wore.

Suspects	Linen	Cotton	Silk	Polyester	Jacket	Pants	Shirt	Vest
Chuck Borinski								
Marvin Muller								
Isabelle Parker								
Ray Slade								
Jacket								
Pants								
Shirt								
Vest								

Clues:
1. One suspect wore either a polyester shirt or cotton pants.
2. Both Chuck and the man who wore linen hated to wear a vest.
3. Ray spilled a cup of coffee on his new pants.

After your investigation, who do you think committed the crime? List all of the evidence that supports the guilt of this suspect.

_____

_____

_____

FORENSIC ARTISTS

A forensic artist makes a drawing of a suspect based on a description given by a witness. Be a forensic artist and draw one or more of the suspects in *The Great Electric Train Robbery* based on the descriptions of each one found below.

Then, draw the suspects in a lineup. Use the statistics below to make a scale drawing on graph paper (six squares = one foot). Color your drawing, using the description as a guide.

Chuck Borinski is 5'11" and weighs 180 pounds. He is completely bald. His blue eyes are far apart and his nose is square like the shape of his face. His eyebrows are brown and thin. He has a huge mole on the bottom of his chin.

Marvin Muller is 6'1" and weighs 200 pounds. He has gray hair that hangs slightly over his ears. His bangs fall down over his forehead into his brown eyes. His nose is long, extending down almost to his upper lip, which forms an almost perfect capital "M" in the center.

Sam Newton is 5'8" and weighs 190 pounds. His blonde hair is cut very short in a buzz cut. He has a small scar on his forehead just above his left eyebrow. His nose is short and squatty. His face is round and plump, his cheeks fat, his lips large and puffy.

Isabelle Parker is 5'9" and weighs 130 pounds. She has large hazel eyes with narrow eyebrows, which aren't quite as red as her hair. Her hair is straight and falls below her shoulders. She parts it in the middle and wears it pulled back behind her ears. Her oval face is covered with light freckles. Her lips are thin and when she smiles, you notice her beautiful teeth.

Ray Slade is 6' and weighs 190 pounds. His brown eyes are small, narrow slits that are close together. His nose is long and narrow like his face. He has thick brown hair with long bangs covering his forehead. He has a moustache, which is pointed on either end. His lips are thin and pale.

Ralph Yonkers is 6'2" and weighs 225 pounds. He has short black hair and a moustache so thick it almost covers his top lip. His black eyebrows are thick as well, with some of the hairs extending into his eyes. His eyes are brown like chocolate. His nose is long and thick with a wart on the very end.

THE PIZZA DELIVERY JOKE MYSTERY

I. | 100 + 40 + 25 =
    | 20+25+60+45+15+45+75+205+95=
    | 20+25+60+45+110+25+90+25+20 =
    | 80+45+130 +5=

II. | 10 + 44 + 10 + 36 + 50 =
    | 46+30+36+26 =
    | 8+10+38+10+36+44+10+38=
    | 2 =
    | 46+30+36+26 =

III.| 45+15+9+36+10=
    | 46+17+13+14+23+50=
    | 45+29+36+25+37=
    | 46+1+27+8+9+35=

IV. | 291+171+241=
    | 191 +71 +42 +
    | 35 + 86 + 174 +193 =
    | 191 +5+ 181 +195 +49=
    | 196 +45 + 195 +197=

TEACHER'S GUIDE: THE PIZZA DELIVERY JOKE MYSTERY

Introduction

The culprit in this mystery is a high school student who played a prank on a fellow student. The detectives in your class will be asked to solve this crime by analyzing evidence associated with the suspects. The evidence includes a school newspaper, a collection of business cards and books found in the suspects' lockers, a soil sample from the suspects lockers, and a secret code.

To introduce the mystery, read The Pizza Delivery Joke Mystery (p. 54) aloud to students.

Solving the Mystery

First, discuss the following questions about the mystery with your students: Who? What? Where? When? Guide students to understand that the six employees of the pizza restaurant are considered to be suspects because they were the only people who had the opportunity to put worms into the pizza box. Hand out The Suspects' Statements (p. 55). Read and discuss who had the opportunity to commit the crime. From this sheet, students should be able to deduce that Penelope Rodriquez and Franklin Hint had no opportunity to commit the crime. Hand out the Detective Notes chart (p. 56). Students will use this worksheet to keep track of the case's evidence. Instruct them to record their findings on the chart provided.

Gathering Evidence

Ask your detectives to think of why someone would have committed this crime. What is the motive in this case? Hand out the copy of Learn More High School News May Edition (p. 57). Explain to students that the school principal provided this copy of the school's newspaper. Ask students what they can determine about motive from this paper. They should deduce that Penelope Rodriquez has no motive.

Tell students that in order to obtain more evidence, detectives searched the remaining four suspects' lockers. Hand out Evidence Found in the Lockers (pp. 58–59) and discuss. What assumptions might be made about each suspect from this evidence? Discuss who the detectives need to question in order to verify that their statements are true.

Explain to students that after questioning friends and family of the suspects, detectives found that each suspect's statement was true. Does this mean that all of the suspects are innocent? Explain to students that more evidence is needed to determine more information about the suspects. Students will next consider the math paper found in the pizza box.

Solving Clues

Hand out More Evidence Found in the Lockers (p. 60). Ask students how this evidence might be relevant to the case. Students should guess that the math paper might be a code, rather than just math problems.

Hand out Math Homework (p. 61), which contains the sheet found in the pizza box. Why might the culprit have put this in the box? Explain to students that sometimes things are not what they seem to be, particularly with evidence like this. This is why it is important for detectives to think outside of the box and consider evidence from different perspectives. What else might this be other than a simple sheet filled with math problems?

After students have reviewed Math Homework and More Evidence Found in the Lockers, what can they determine about the suspects? They should be keeping notes in the evidence log. Discuss their notes, or let students compare their answers.

Then, ask students if they can eliminate anyone from the suspect list. Students should eliminate Wanda Wallace, because according to the evidence, she struggles with math. The code found in the pizza box focuses on math, so it is unlikely that she would have made up the math sheet.

Now instruct students to try and decipher the code. Direct them to find the numbers that are most frequently used in the problems in the first row. In the first row, 25 is the most frequently used number. Explain that they might try substituting 25 for E. Then, ask them try to figure out the sequence of numbers in these problems. (They should notice that the numbers are all divisible by five, so the pattern is based on five.) Ask your students, if E equals the number 25, then what number would A be? Or B? And, so on? Have your students figure out the rest of the numbers and decipher the code on the first row of problems.

Follow the same procedure for the second row of problems. If your students have difficulty, hand out the Code Deciphering Key (p. 62) and explain that a detective found this under a table in the locker room. It had no marks indicating its owner. Using this key, the students will be able to decipher all of the codes.

Ask your students the following questions: Why might the suspect have put this coded message in the pizza box? Which suspect becomes highly suspicious as the culprit once you determine that the code was based on numbers? Is this enough evidence to prove this suspect is guilty? Students should answer that, no, this isn't enough evidence to prove the suspect's guilt—more evidence is needed to confirm.

Explain to students that in addition to the paper evidence that they've reviewed, traces of dirt were found in three of the suspects' lockers, belonging to Olivia, Harold, and Oscar. No traces of soil were found in Wanda's locker. Ask your students: What does the fact that no soil was found indicate about Wanda's innocence or guilt?

Hand out the Soil Analysis Chart (p. 63). How can the facts on this chart help students solve this crime? If you wish to pose a greater challenge to your students, incorporate the hands-on activity Soil Analysis Chart #2 (pp. 64–65; see description below). This activity requires students to test and analyze soil samples from the crime scene.

Based on this evidence, whom can students name as the culprit? After discussing your students' outcome of the crime, read the Conclusion to this mystery to students. Use the Answer Key to check over your student's work.

Optional Activity

In preparation for this optional activity, ask three students to bring in a plastic bag or coffee can filled with dirt that they collected from their backyard. Or, you can gather the dirt from three different locations on the school grounds. Put the dirt from the first location into three different gallon-size freezer bags or coffee cans. Label them as follows: Tony's Catch All Bait Shop; pizza box; Harold's locker. Put the dirt found in the second location into two different freezer bags. Label these bags: Cast-a-Line Tackle & Bait Shop; Olivia's locker. Put the dirt from the third location into one freezer bag. Label this bag: Oscar's locker. For this activity you will need the following materials for each pair of students:

- a 100-ml measuring cup (to make these yourself, measure 3 ounces of water, plus 2 teaspoons of water, and pour into a small plastic cup. Mark the water level with a permanent marker, labeling it 100 ml);
- a centimeter ruler;
- 6 Styrofoam cups;
- 6 large plastic cups;
- large paper clips; and
- water.

Tell students that they are going to act like forensic scientists and analyze and compare the dirt found in the pizza box, with a sample from the worm box, the bait shops, and with the traces of dirt found in the suspects' lockers.

Students will need to select a partner, or you can separate students into small groups. Then, hand out the Soil Analysis Chart #2 (pp. 63) and tell students that after recording their observations of each sample, they are to follow the procedure on the following page in order to conduct the water-holding capacity test. Hand out supplies to each group. After they record their observations and complete the test, ask them to compare the soil samples with the soil found on the pizza. Discuss their results together as a class.

Conclusion

After considering the soil evidence, the detectives confronted Harold. The boy broke down and confessed that he had doctored the pizza. "It was only a joke," he said. "I'm so sorry for all the trouble that I caused. I guess I was really jealous of Ronald." Harold explained to detectives that he had put the worms into the pizza when Olivia was getting another order ready for delivery. He knew that Ronald always ordered a pizza on Friday night and he had purchased the worms Friday afternoon at the bait shop and carried them to work, storing them in his locker until Ronald's pizza was hot and in the box. "I realize I was wrong and will take responsibility for my actions." He agreed to buy 20 pizzas for Ronald.

Answer Key

Suspects' Statements

Penelope Rodriquez and Franklin Hint had no opportunity to commit the crime.

Learn More School News

Penelope Rodriquez had no motive. All other suspects had a motive.

Evidence Found in Lockers

All evidence indicates each suspect might be guilty.

More Evidence Found in Lockers

The letter to Wanda's mother indicates Wanda has difficulty in math. As a result of this, it is improbable that she would have put the coded math sheet in the pizza box. She is, therefore, an unlikely culprit.

Math Homework Code

I. The delicious delivered pizza; II. Every worm deserves a worm; III. Where wiggly worms wander; IV. Try the dirt taste test.

Soil Analysis Chart

The soil in Harold's locker matches the soil found in the pizza box.

THE PIZZA DELIVERY JOKE MYSTERY

Ronald McDonaldson, a student at Learn More High School, recently received quite a jolt when he ordered a pizza from Deliver-It-To-You Pizza. The delivery girl, Olivia Cashdollar, brought the super large pizza exactly 20 minutes after he called in the order. Ronald set the pizza on the kitchen table and eagerly opened the box. He was surprised to find a sheet of paper filled with math problems lying on top of the pizza. Puzzled, he lifted the paper and was shocked at the awful sight—Instead of his favorite pepperoni pizza topped with triple cheese, he found a pizza topped with 10 squirmy worms.

Irate, he called Deliver-It-To-You Pizza. "What is this?" he shouted. Then, he described the pizza he had received to the manager, Lucy Goodfellow. "I have no idea what's going on," she said, "but I'll get to the bottom of this."

After talking with Ronald, Lucy Goodfellow called in her six employees and told them about Ronald's pizza. All of them appeared to be surprised. She then called a detective to help her figure out who tainted the pizza. Help her get to the bottom of this squirmy crime!

THE SUSPECTS' STATEMENTS

As detective on this case, your first priority was to question the pizza shop employees about the wormy pizza. Analyze the statements below to see if any suspects can be eliminated.

"How could that have happened?" Harold Flowerdew asked. "I cooked his pizza. It was fine when I gave it to Oscar to put into the box."

"Harold took that pizza out as I put another one in," Wanda Wallace said. "It looked OK to me then."

"What I boxed up was definitely a pepperoni pizza," Oscar Stillwell said.

"Well, I never opened that box," Olivia Cashdollar stated.

"I never would have done such a thing," Penelope Rodriquez said. "Especially since I planned to go to Ronald's after work and eat some of the pizza he ordered."

"I think it's disgusting someone put worms on that pizza," Franklin Hint said. "One of my prize pizzas. The one with triple cheese! What a waste!"

Detectives then asked the suspects if they noticed anyone acting suspiciously right after Ronald's pizza was made and before Olivia Cashdollar picked it up for delivery.

"Wanda Wallace had a sneezing spell right after I boxed Ronald's pizza," Oscar said. "She asked if I had a tissue and I went to my locker for a minute to get her one, leaving the pizza right there, alone."

"Just when I was getting into my car to take the pizza, Harold stuck his head out the door and told me that Oscar wanted to see me," Olivia said. "When I went inside and asked Oscar what he wanted, he looked at me like I was crazy."

"I didn't notice anything," Franklin said. "I was so busy making up two pizzas that I didn't have time to look up."

"I didn't notice anyone but Franklin way back in the kitchen, creating another of his famous pizzas," Olivia said. "Penelope was in the storage room, stacking up canned tomatoes."

Based on the suspects' statements, can you eliminate any suspects?

_____

Name:_____ Date:_____

DETECTIVE NOTES

After questioning Deliver-It-To-You Pizza manager, Lucy Goodfellow, you made a chart and jotted down the following facts about each of the five employees. As you uncover more clues, record your findings on the chart.

Suspects	Motive — Write Yes or No for each suspect's motive based on the clues listed below.			Opportunity — Write Yes or No for each suspect's opportunity based on the clues listed below.	
	Clue #1	Clue #2	Clue #3	Clue #1	Clue #2
Employee Information	Student Newspaper	Business Cards	Notes Found in Locker	Suspects' Statements	Soil Analysis
Olivia Cashdollar 18 years old 12th grader at Learn More High School Worked at pizza place for 2 years					
Oscar Stillwell 17 years old 11th grader at Learn More High School Worked at pizza place for 10 months					
Harold Flowerdew 17 years old 11th grader at Learn More High School Worked at pizza place for one year					
Wanda Wallace 16 years old 11th grader at Learn More High School Worked at pizza place for one month					
Penelope Rodriguez 17 years old 11th grader at Learn More High School Worked at pizza place for 8 months					
Franklin Hint 18 years old 12th grader at Learn More High School Worked at pizza place for 18 months					

LEARN MORE HIGH SCHOOL NEWS
MAY EDITION

Your next step in solving this case is to determine the culprit's motivation to taint the pizza. The suspects' school principal gave you a recent copy of their school's newspaper. Read through the newspaper articles and take note of any possible clues that may suggest the culprit's motive. Is there any suspect whom you can eliminate from the list because he or she has no motive, according to the articles?

LEARN MORE HIGH SCHOOL NEWS
May Edition

THREE JUNIORS ELECTED STUDENT COUNCIL OFFICERS

The student council recently held its election of officers for the upcoming school year. Ronald McDonaldson was elected president of the organization. His opponent, Wanda Wallace, congratulated Ronald after the election results were announced. The new officers will be installed at an assembly program next Friday.

Recently elected officers: (from left) President Ronald McDonaldson; Treasurer, Penelope Rodriguez; and Vice President, Oscar Stillwell.

SWIM MEET

A swim meet was held on May 21 in Learn More's new indoor swimming pool. The swim team's prize swimmer, Ronald McDonaldson, came in first in the following events: freestyle, backstroke, sidestroke, and the butterfly stroke. Oscar Stillwell placed second in the freestyle event.

SPRING BAND CONCERT

The annual spring band concert was held May 14. Under the direction of Mr. Herbert Gathright, the band performed many delightful show tunes. The highlight was a trumpet duet by first chair, Ronald McDonaldson, and second chair, Harold Flowerdew.

STUDENT WINS NATIONAL MATH COMPETITION

Ronald McDonaldson won the state math competition last week. After winning the county competition in April, the 11th grader went to the state meet last Thursday. Harold Flowerdew was the runner-up at the county competition. We congratulate both of these talented math students.

SUPPORT THE BAND CAKE SALE

The band will hold its annual cake sale this Saturday at the Hometown Mall. The proceeds from the sale will help finance the summer band camp held in August. Plan to come to the sale and support your band. The cakes are delicious!

JUNIOR PROM QUEEN & KING ANNOUNCED

The Student Council announced yesterday that Ronald McDonaldson and Penelope Rodriguez were elected Junior Prom King and Queen after tallying last Friday's vote. They will preside at the Junior Prom on June 1 at the Fireman's Hall. The couple will kick off the event by dancing the first dance. They will retain their crown through the fall semester of next year and will serve as the King and Queen of next year's Homecoming. Congratulations to this royal couple!

EVIDENCE FOUND IN THE LOCKERS

In order to obtain more evidence, detectives searched each of the four suspects' lockers. They found a business card in each suspects' locker. Study each card carefully, and determine how these cards might be relevant to the case.

Found in Olivia Cashdollar's locker

Found in Harold Flowerdew's locker

Found in Oscar Stillwell's locker

Found in Wanda Wallace's locker

Catch-a-Line Tackle
725-7068
Ask for Harry

Detectives make assumptions about their cases based on the evidence they uncover. An assumption is a fact that is believed to be true, and therefore conclusions can be made from this fact. Detectives might assume that Olivia Cashdollar purchased worms because she had a business card in her locker from a bait shop. Two other suspects, however, had evidence in their lockers that indicated they had knowledge of a bait shop, as well. Detectives can't assume, therefore, that Olivia is the culprit. The other two suspects also could be guilty.

And, what about the card found in Stillwell's locker? How does this relate to the case? What assumptions might you make about Stillwell?

_____

_____

_____

_____

EVIDENCE FOUND IN THE LOCKERS

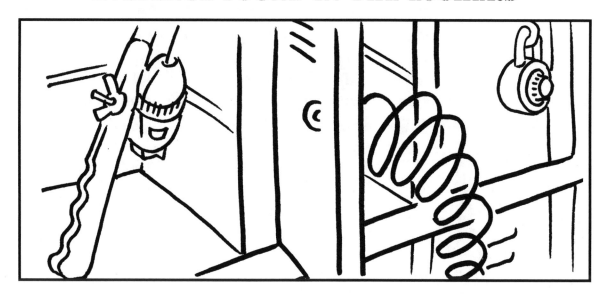

Detectives must gather more information. Otherwise, they might make a false assumption—one that is not based on enough facts. A valid assumption is one that can be substantiated or backed up with sufficient evidence. In order to get more information, you questioned the suspects to find out why they had these items in their locker. These were their statements:

Olivia Cashdollar: "My father loves to fish and my Mom and I bought him a new fishing pole for his birthday."

Harold Flowerdew: "My Dad and I are planning a fishing trip and I needed some new lines for my fishing gear."

Wanda Wallace: "My brother asked me to stop by last week and pick up the new rod and reel he had ordered."

Oscar Stillwell: "My friend works at this shop and gave me his business card."

In order to make valid assumptions based on personal statements, detectives need to validate or substantiate each statement as the truth. Who might you question to verify that the above statements are true?

_____

_____

_____

_____

MORE EVIDENCE FOUND IN THE LOCKERS

You also found these items in the suspects' lockers. Examine each one carefully. How might these items be related to the case? In order to determine this, you considered the other evidence found in the pizza box, particularly the math sheet. Can you eliminate a suspect from your suspect list because of information you found in one of these suspects' lockers?

Note found in Wanda's locker

Dear Mrs. Wallace,

I am concerned about Wanda's grades in my Algebra class. She told me that she had always struggled with math. Perhaps you might consider hiring a tutor for her. She said that she thought this would be a good idea. Please give me a call and we can discuss it.

Thanks,
Mrs. Marshall

Assignment book found in Oscar's locker

```
American History
Assignment

Ms. Ramez's class

Research secret codes.
Then, select a specific
type of code & write a
message for a friend to
decipher. Provide a key
as a guide.

Due: May 26
```

Class schedule found in Olivia's locker

LEARN MORE HIGH SCHOOL
Class Schedule

Student: Olivia Cashdollar

Period 1 - Calculus
  Mrs. Harrod
Period 2 - English Lit
  Mr. Williams
Period 3 – Band
  Mr. Gathright
Period 4 - Latin
  Ms. McKnuckle
Period 5 - American History
  Ms. Ramez
Period 6 - Chemistry
  Ms. Simon

Paperback book found in Harold's locker

An Introduction to Codes, Ciphers and Cryptograms

By Willard Hysong

Name:_____ Date:_____

MATH HOMEWORK

Examine this assignment sheet carefully. How might items in the suspects' lockers be connected to this homework? How are the books found in Harold and Oscar's lockers relevant to the case? Which item provides a clue that points to one suspect who most likely did not commit the crime? What do you think the relevance of this homework is to the mystery?

_____

_____

_____

I.	$100 + 40 + 25 =$
	$20 + 25 + 60 + 45 + 15 + 45 + 75 + 105 + 95 =$
	$20 + 25 + 60 + 45 + 110 + 25 + 90 + 25 + 20 =$
	$80 + 45 + 130 + 5 =$
II.	$10 + 44 + 10 + 36 + 50 =$
	$46 + 30 + 36 + 26 =$
	$8 + 10 + 38 + 10 + 36 + 44 + 10 + 38 =$
	$2 =$
	$46 + 30 + 36 + 26 =$
III.	$45 + 15 + 9 + 36 + 10 =$
	$46 + 17 + 13 + 14 + 23 + 50 =$
	$45 + 29 + 36 + 25 + 37 =$
	$46 + 1 + 27 + 8 + 9 + 35 =$
IV.	$191 + 171 + 241 =$
	$191 + 71 + 42 +$
	$35 + 86 + 174 + 193 =$
	$191 + 5 + 181 + 195 + 49 =$
	$196 + 45 + 185 + 197 =$

CODE DECIPHERING KEY

If you figured out the math sheet was really a code, you were right. And, if you determined that Wanda Wallace probably didn't have anything to do with a math paper and therefore wasn't a likely culprit, you are right about that, too.

After discovering that the math sheet is actually a code, you find a deciphering key balled up in a trashcan near the lockers in the pizza place. Use the key to crack the code. Frequency of a letter, number, or symbol in a code is a clue to how to decipher the code. The letters *E* and *T* are the most frequently used letters in the English language. *A, O, N, I, R*, and *S* are used frequently, as well. More than half of the words in the English language end in *E, S, D*, or *T*. More than half of the words begin with *T, A, O, S*, or *W*.

Row I		Row II		Row III		Row IV	
A	5	A	2	A	1–2	A	1–10
B	10	B	4	B	3–4	B	11–20
C	15	C	6	C	5–6	C	21–30
D	20	D	8	D	7–8	D	31–40
E	25	E	10	E	9–10	E	41–50
F	30	F	12	F	11–12	F	51–60
G	35	G	14	G	13–14	G	61–70
H	40	H	16	H	15–16	H	71–80
I	45	I	18	I	17–18	I	81–90
J	50	J	20	J	19–20	J	91–100
K	55	K	22	K	21–22	K	101–110
L	60	L	24	L	23–24	L	111–120
M	65	M	26	M	25–26	M	121–130
N	70	N	28	N	27–28	N	131–140
O	75	O	30	O	29–30	O	141–150
P	80	P	32	P	31–32	P	151–160
Q	85	Q	34	Q	33–34	Q	161–170
R	90	R	36	R	35–36	R	171–180
S	95	S	38	S	37–38	S	181–190
T	100	T	40	T	39–40	T	191–200
U	105	U	42	U	41–42	U	201–210
V	110	V	44	V	43–44	V	211–220
W	115	W	46	W	45–46	W	221–230
X	120	X	48	X	47–48	X	231–240
Y	125	Y	50	Y	49–50	Y	241–250
Z	130	Z	52	Z	51–52	Z	251–260

SOIL ANALYSIS CHART

After cracking the code, you take one final look at the lockers at the pizza shop. There you notice something strange—three of the lockers contain traces of dirt. Compare the dirt found in the lockers to the samples from the bait shop and the crime scene.

Sample Labels	Location Of Sample	Color	Texture: Fine, Medium, or Coarse	Natural and/or Man-Made Objects Found in Sample
Crime Scene	Pizza Box	Dark Brown	Coarse	None
Sample A	Cast-a-Line Tackle & Bait Shop	Light Brown	Fine	None
Sample B	Tony's Catch All Bait Shop	Dark Brown	Coarse	None
Locker 1	Oscar's Locker	Dark Brown	Medium	Small Pebbles
Locker 2	Olivia's Locker	Light Brown	Coarse	Tiny Pieces of Cement
Locker 3	Harold's Locker	Dark Brown	Coarse	None

Examine the above chart carefully. What soil found in the lockers and the bait shops matched the soil found in the pizza box?

_____

Based on all of the evidence that you have collected, who do you think is the culprit? List all of the evidence that supports the guilt of this suspect.

_____

_____

_____

_____

_____

_____

SOIL ANALYSIS CHART #2

After cracking the code, you take one final look at the lockers at the pizza shop. There you notice something strange—three of the lockers contain traces of dirt. Use the chart below and the samples provided by your teacher to determine which sample found in the lockers matches that found at the crime scene.

Examine each sample carefully with a magnifying lens and record your findings on the chart.

Sample Labels	Location of Sample	Color	Texture: Fine, Medium, Coarse	Natural and/or Man-Made Objects Found in Sample	Water Holding Capacity	Water Level in Cup After 5 Minutes
Crime Scene	Pizza Box					
Sample A	Cast-a-Line Tackle & Bait Shop					
Sample B	Tony's Catch All Bait Shop					
Locker 1	Oscar's Locker					
Locker 2	Olivia's Locker					
Locker 3	Harold's Locker					

SOIL ANALYSIS CHART #2

Then, follow this procedure to determine the water-holding capacity of each sample.

1. Your teacher will provide you with the following: a large paper clip, a centimeter ruler, 100-ml measuring cup, water, six regular-sized plastic cups labeled with the words found in the first column on the Soil Analysis Chart #2, six large plastic cups, and six Styrofoam cups. You or your teacher should label the Styrofoam cups, using the labels found in the first column on the Soil Analysis Chart #2.

2. Use the end of the paper clip to poke one hole in the bottom of each Styrofoam cup in its center.

3. Get soil from one of the large freezer bags. Note its label. Put the soil in the 2 oz. cup corresponding to this label. Fill it to the very top. Find the Styrofoam cup with the corresponding label. Put the soil in the Styrofoam cup. Hold this cup above the large plastic cup. Then, add 2 oz. of water into the dirt.

4. Time the number of seconds it takes for the water to begin to drip through the hole on the bottom of the Styrofoam cup into the plastic cup. Record on the chart. After the water has begun to drip, place the Styrofoam cup inside the plastic cup.

5. Repeat the test, using another soil sample. Continue until you have tested all six samples.

6. Five minutes after you test each sample, measure the water level in the plastic cup, using the milliliter ruler. Record your findings on the chart.

Did you match the soil found in the pizza box with the soil found in the suspects' lockers? If so, what does this match suggest? Based on this evidence, who do you think the culprit is?

_____

_____

_____

_____

_____

_____

STEALING THE SPOTLIGHT

TEACHER'S GUIDE: STEALING THE SPOTLIGHT

Introduction

A stage is the setting for this theatrical crime, where someone attempts to keep the famous stage actress, Veronica Best, from delivering her lines. Student detectives will review the evidence found by the chief detective assigned to the case. In addition, students will become crime scene investigators and analyze the evidence found at the crime scene.

Solving the Mystery

Ask students to read Stealing the Spotlight (p. 72), which introduces the case. Then, discuss the following questions about the crime: What happened? Who was the intended victim? Who are the most likely suspects? Students should be able to deduce that members of the cast and crew are the most likely suspects.

Hand out The Suspect List (pp. 73–74). Ask students why someone might have done this. Discuss a possible motive. Ask students if any suspects can be eliminated due to a lack of motive, according to the evidence you have gathered. They should be able to deduce that the stage manager did not have a motive for committing the crime.

The next question students need to answer is when the crime took place. Explain to them that determining when the crime took place will narrow the suspect list to name only those who had the opportunity to commit the crime. Hand out Suspect Alibis (pp. 75–76). Discuss which suspect had an alibi that was substantiated, or backed-up by someone else.

Students next need to see where the crime took place. Explain that detectives use the clues they find at the crime scene to reconstruct the crime. Hand out the Crime Scene Sketch (p. 77). Ask students to examine it carefully and answer the questions below about the crime based on the clues found at the crime scene.

1. How did the culprit enter the theatre?
2. When did the culprit probably get the key out of the desk?
3. How did the culprit weaken the scenic baton?
4. What caused the blood stains at the crime scene?
5. Why is there a concentration of bloodstains in only one section of the stage?
6. Why isn't there blood near the middle and right ropes that held the baton, or anywhere else on the stage?

Gathering Evidence

Hand out the Bloodstain Analysis sheet (p. 78). Explain that this is a resource students can use to determine the height and angle from which the blood fell onto the stage at the crime scene. After they read the sheet, discuss the relationship between the height from which blood was dropped and the size of the stain that it leaves. *As the height increases, the size of the drop increases.*

Next, discuss how the impact angle affects the stain. *As the impact angle decreases, the bloodstains become elongated.* Point out that as the angle decreases, the more secondary splashes form away around the primary drop. These secondary splashes always move in the same direction in which the blood was dropped. This fact helps detectives determine the location from which the blood fell. You may want to sketch examples of these details on a chalkboard, or somewhere visible to students. Ask them several examples, to make sure that they understand the relationship between height and angle of a blood drop.

Hand out Crime Scene Bloodstains (p. 79). Instruct students to estimate the angle and height from which the blood was dropped at the crime scene.

Tell students that they will now gather more evidence by solving two matrix logic puzzles. Hand out the puzzles Cuts and Abrasions and I Couldn't Climb That Ladder (p. 80 and pp. 81–82), and ask students to find the solutions. Discuss why this evidence is important to the case.

Hand out the DNA Analysis sheet (p. 86) and ask students to compare the DNA found in the blood on the stage with the DNA of each of the suspects. The result of this analysis will provide the evidence to prove that one of the suspects is the culprit. You also may want to explain the significance of DNA testing to your students. Tell students that DNA testing can prove beyond a doubt that a suspect is guilty or innocent. In some cases DNA testing has proved a convicted criminal's innocence years after a crime was committed. Use the information box (see Figure 1) to give more specified information if necessary.

Ask the students to compile all of the evidence and identify the culprit.

Optional Activity

In this lab, students will use simulated blood to create bloodstains dropped from different heights and angles. Hand out the Forensics Lab sheet (pp. 83–84). Have students work in groups of two or three and complete the activities. Ask the groups to compare their findings. To extend this activity, you might ask students to determine if the surface on which blood is dropped affects the stain. Have them drop blood on a variety of surfaces, such as a scrap piece of carpet, wax paper, poster

- DNA is used to help identify missing persons and was very beneficial in determining the identity of the victims of the World Trade Center attack on 9/11.
- DNA can prove beyond a doubt that a suspect is guilty, even in crimes that cross state lines. In 2002, DNA proved that a man had committed crimes in both Pennsylvania and Colorado.
- DNA also can prove that a person convicted of a crime is innocent, sometimes years after the crime was committed. In 2003, a Virginia man was exonerated and released from prison when DNA tests proved that he was not the perpetrator of a crime committed in 1981.
- The DNA Identification Act of 1994 gave the FBI the authority to establish a DNA database (CODIS, Combined DNA Index System). This database contains a DNA profile of known criminals in all 50 states. When DNA is found at a crime scene, it is compared to DNA listed in the database. This helps authorities identify serial criminals, as well as those who commit crimes across state lines.
- DNA can identify the remains of someone who died long ago. In 1998, the soldier buried in the Tomb of the Unknown Soldier was identified as a result of DNA testing. This soldier, Michael Blassie, was killed in Vietnam in 1972.
- DNA also can be used to prevent fraud. Using DNA technology, the NFL tagged all of the footballs used in the 34th Super Bowl to prevent someone in the future from selling an ordinary ball, claiming it was used in the game.

Figure 1. DNA testing: Background information.

board, or a piece of cotton cloth. In lieu of student participation, you might choose to demonstrate this lab.

To prepare for this optional lab, gather the following supplies for each group of students:

- a copy of angle patterns from the Pattern Pieces sheet (p. 85),
- scissors,
- 20+ index cards (5" x 7"),
- a medicine dropper,
- a small plastic cup filled with fake blood,
- a plastic garbage bag, and
- a tape measure.

To make the activity more time efficient, you may wish to cut the pattern pieces and separate the different angles into stations that students can rotate and use. In this case, you would only need to fold and cut one set of pattern pieces (or you could double the set and have two stations of each angle measurement if you have a large classroom). This would furthermore save you from providing index cards for individuals to cut and use.

To complete the set-up of this activity, you will also need to make the simulated blood, using the recipe found in Figure 2.

Ingredients:

- 4 Tb cornstarch
- ⅔ cup water
- ⅔ cup corn syrup
- 3–5 drops red food coloring
- 2–3 drops green food coloring
- White glue (such as Elmer's brand glue)
- plastic disposable container
- plastic cups

Directions:

Put water in a plastic, disposable container. Add cornstarch. Mix well. Add corn syrup. Mix again. Place 3–4 teaspoons of this mixture into a plastic cup. Add 3–5 drops red food coloring. Add 2–3 drops green food coloring. Stir well. Now, add glue until the mixture thickens. The blood needs to be thicker than water, but not as thick as pudding. If it gets too thick, add some of the first mixture from the plastic container. You can also add more corn syrup to make it smooth. Experiment until you get it just right.

Figure 2. Recipe for simulated blood.

Conclusion

When confronted with the evidence, Grace St. James broke down and sobbed. "Yes! Yes! Yes!" she cried, "I did it. I didn't mean for Veronica to get hurt badly. I just wanted to frighten her so she wouldn't want to continue on in the play. I am so tired of people never noticing me when I'm on stage. All eyes are always on Veronica. I'm so sorry. I was very wrong. And, I know that I will have to pay for this stupid action. I know that bad deeds always lead to consequences."

Answer Key

Crime Scene Sketch Questions

1. The culprit took the key from the desk drawer.
2. The culprit probably took the key during rehearsal and returned to the theatre after the stage manager left at 4:45 p.m. for dinner. If this is true, it confirms that the culprit was a member of the cast or crew.

3. The culprit cut each of the three braided ropes, leaving a single strand on each rope to hold the baton. The single strands weren't strong enough to support the baton when it was lowered.
4. The culprit probably cut him- or herself with the razor blade when cutting the rope.
5. The culprit must have cut rope #1, then #2, before cutting himself at rope #3. This would explain why there would not have been blood near the first two ropes.
6. The culprit wrapped the wound with something to stop the bleeding, therefore the blood no longer dripped.

Crime Scene Bloodstains

Angles: #1—90°; #2—10°; #3—70°; #4—30°; #5—50°. Heights: #6—1 ft; #7—1 ft; #8—6 in; #9—4 ft; #10—8 ft.

Cuts and Abrasions

Theodore Newman, cut, chin; Jamison Lively, scab, right ankle; Grace St. James, Band-Aid, left index finger; Allison Loveall, bruise, right arm; Madison Kane, bandage, left elbow.

I Couldn't Climb That Ladder

Theodore Newman, vertigo, Dr. Gice, e-mail; Jamison Lively, fear of ladders, Dr. Law, text message; Grace St. James, fear of heights, Dr. Fill, no phone/address; Madison Kane, knee problem, Dr. Sam, phone.

STEALING THE SPOTLIGHT

The Travel Theatre Company began its first performance of the play *Murder at Eight* last evening at the Center Theatre in Center City. During the performance, the scenic baton fell onto the stage and trapped Veronica Best, the leading lady, beneath it. Veronica was critically injured and taken to the hospital where she was treated for a broken leg and a mild concussion. She will be unable to continue the tour.

The scenic baton is a heavy wooden pole suspended from the ceiling by three large ropes. The baton stretches across the back of the stage. Backdrops for theatrical productions are painted on large sheets of canvas, and then attached to the baton and wrapped around it. The canvas can be raised and lowered like a window shade. The baton also can be lowered when it is necessary to change backdrops.

The *Murder at Eight* play utilized the scenic baton, and Veronica Best was the only actor in the play who would stand directly under the scenic baton during the performance. As written in the script, she said the following line: "The baton. A perfect murder weapon, weighing almost a ton." As she said this line, she stepped back as directed and stood beneath the baton, extending her arm above her head. This line was the cue for the stage manager to slowly lower the baton. Last night when the manager began to lower the baton, it fell. She screamed when it crashed to the ground. At first, the audience laughed, thinking it was part of the play. But, when several members of the cast began yelling for someone to call an ambulance, the audience was silenced.

The stage manager said that she checked the stage just before she left for dinner to make certain everything was in order for the night's performance. She even lowered the baton and raised it back up to make certain it was in the right position. Everything was as it should be.

You were recently appointed to Lead Assistant Detective, so it's your job to assist real-life detective Amy Waldrop in the solving of the Stealing the Spotlight mystery.

Name:_____ Date:_____

THE SUSPECT LIST

After she was assigned to the case, Detective Amy Waldrop talked with members of the cast and crew of the Travel Theatre Company. Read the notes she took about each member. What can you determine about the motive for this crime from this information?

Theodore Newman, director:

Newman was a successful director until his last two plays flopped. As a result, he was unable to obtain work until 8 months ago when he was hired to direct *Murder at Eight* for the Travel Theatre Company. Several members of the crew claimed that Newman and Veronica Best started arguing the first day of rehearsals and have continued doing so throughout the production. "Yesterday, they really had it out," the stage manager said. "Veronica told him he was the worst director she had ever seen and that she was going to ask the producer to get rid of him."

Jamison Lively, leading male actor:

Lively has been touring with The Travel Theatre Company. for the last 5 years. He has always received top billing until this production. Veronica Best, an actress frequently seen in *PEOPLE* magazine, agreed to star in the production only if she had top billing and was allowed to appear alone at all of the interviews promoting the production at local TV stations.

Grace St. James, supporting actress:

St. James has worked with Veronica in several productions. She auditioned for the leading role in three of the last plays they did together, including *Murder at Eight*. Veronica always won the lead. St. James made no secret of her jealousy. "Just because she's always got her name in the news doesn't mean she's more talented than I am," she recently said.

THE SUSPECT LIST

Allison Loveall, understudy for Veronica Best:

Loveall has been Veronica's understudy for 6 years. "Always the bridesmaid, never the bride," she frequently joked. The director, however, said Loveall really didn't think it was a joke. "She told me just the other day that she was losing patience with her career. She said she was tired of this role."

Iris Stone, stage manager:

Stone has been stage manager for the last three plays produced by the Travel Theatre Company. "I am thrilled to be involved in this play," she said. "It's such a privilege to work with a great star like Veronica."

Madison Kane, lighting director:

Kane has worked with Veronica Best on several other productions. "The last time I worked with her, I swore I'd never do it again," Kane told the stage manager. "She's always complained about the lighting, claiming that it makes her look bad. She acted like I didn't know what I was doing."

Bret Woods, sound director:

Woods had recently been hired to direct the sound for the Travel Theatre Company. "I am so excited about this job," he told Madison. "The only thorn is Veronica Best. She thinks she's too good to speak to me. She acts like I'm not even here."

Write down your suspicions of possible motives for each suspect in your notes.

SUSPECT ALIBIS

Next, Detective Waldrop focused on when the crime occurred and she interviewed the suspects to determine where they were at the time the crime was committed. Read her notes, and take notes of your own.

The touring group arrived in Center City on Tuesday evening. They had a rehearsal Wednesday afternoon from 2 p.m. until 3:45 p.m. All of the cast and crew, except the stage manager, left the theatre at 4 p.m. The stage manager left at 4:45 p.m. Everyone returned to the theatre at 6 p.m. to get ready for the 7:30 p.m. performance. The baton fell at 8:00 p.m.

Detectives asked the stage manager if she had seen anyone in the theatre between 4 and 4:45 p.m. "Not a soul," she said. "And, I'm certain of that because I spent the entire time working at the desk located on stage right wing. I would have seen somebody if they had been on the stage."

When asked where they were between 4:45 p.m. and 6 p.m. before the performance, the suspects gave the following statements:

Theodore Newman: "Iris Stone met me for dinner at the Blue Bird Restaurant at 4:45 p.m. We ran into Bret Woods there and he joined us. We all walked back to the theatre around 6. It's right next door to the restaurant."

Jamison Lively: "I had a terrible headache and went directly to the hotel after rehearsal. I rested until it was time to come to the theatre."

Grace St. James: "I went back to the hotel and rehearsed my lines. I was having trouble with the second act and wanted to go over it one more time."

Allison Loveall: "I went shopping at the new mall but I didn't buy anything."

Madison Kane: "I was supposed to meet Bret for dinner but instead I was sound asleep in my room at the hotel and didn't wake up until 5:45 p.m. I really had to hurry to make it to the theatre in time but I got there exactly at 6 p.m."

Bret Woods: "I went to dinner at the Blue Bird Restaurant next to the theatre. I was planning to meet Madison there but she never showed up so I ate with Theo and Iris. We left to go back to the theatre just before 6."

SUSPECT ALIBIS

Notes to Substantiate the Suspects' Alibis

The hostess at the Blue Bird Restaurant said that she remembered seeing Theodore Newman and a woman in the restaurant. When asked about Bret Woods, she said that he had told her he was meeting a friend. "Whoever it was, never showed up," she said, "so he sat with Mr. Newman. They all left together around 6 p.m."

The cast and crew of the Traveling Theatre Company were staying at the Rex Hotel located two blocks from the theatre. The woman at the desk remembered seeing Jamison Lively in the lobby a little after 4 but didn't see him after that. And, she didn't see Grace St. James or Madison Kane. Neither did any of the other hotel employees.

Detectives questioned employees at the new mall. No one remembered seeing Allison Loveall.

Did any of the suspects have an alibi that could be substantiated (backed up)?

_____

_____

_____

_____

CRIME SCENE SKETCH

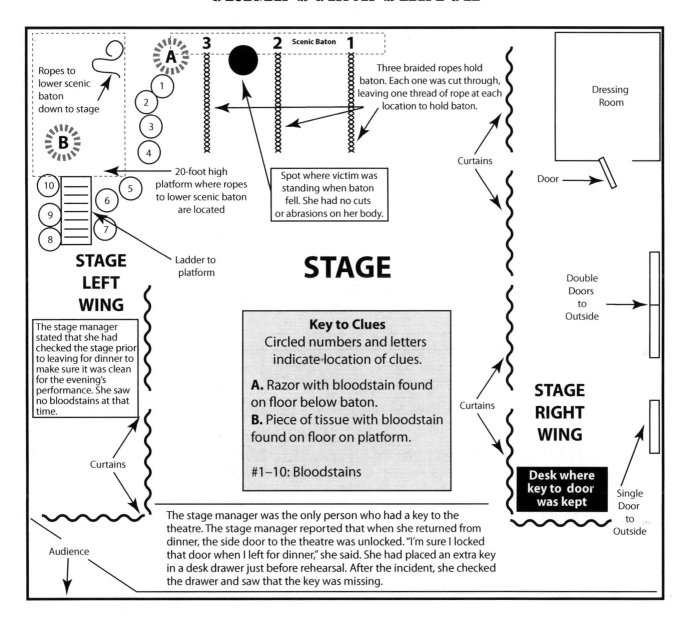

Detective Waldrop then considered evidence found at the crime scene. Examine the Crime Scene Sketch and answer the following questions based on this evidence:

1. How did the culprit enter the theatre?
2. When did the culprit probably get the key out of the desk?
3. How did the culprit weaken the scenic baton?
4. What caused the blood stains at the crime scene?
5. Why is there a concentration of bloodstains in only one section of the stage?
6. Why isn't there blood near the middle and right ropes that held the baton, or anywhere else on the stage?

BLOODSTAIN ANALYSIS

Forensic scientists examined all of the bloodstains found at the crime scene. Based on the shape and size of the each stain, they can determine the height and the angle from which the blood fell.

The height from which blood is dropped affects it size. Examine these bloodstains. They each fell from the same angle but from different heights. What do you notice about their sizes in relation to the height from which each drop fell?

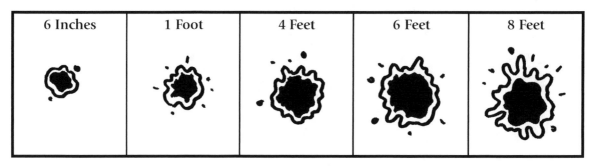

| 6 Inches | 1 Foot | 4 Feet | 6 Feet | 8 Feet |

An average drop of blood contains .05 ml of liquid. The average speed at which a drop falls is 25.1 feet per second. When the height is increased, the speed increases. This increase in speed affects the force of the impact when the blood makes contact with a surface. The greater impact causes the drop to spread out, making it appear to be larger on the surface.

The impact angle affects the shape of a blood drop. Examine these bloodstains. They each fell from the same height but from a different angle. What do you notice about the shape of these stains in relation to the angle from which each one fell?

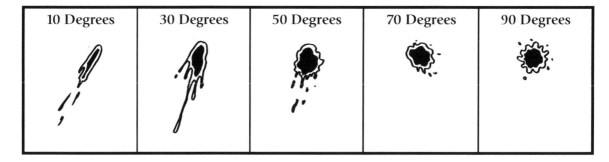

| 10 Degrees | 30 Degrees | 50 Degrees | 70 Degrees | 90 Degrees |

The angle from which a drop of blood falls is called the *impact angle*. Someone bleeding might drip blood from a 90-degree angle directly down onto the floor. But, if the person is lifting his hand, the blood might drip on the floor from a lower angle such as 70 degrees. Or, it might be as low of an angle as 50 or 10 degrees. The angle depends on the tilt of the hand in relation to the surface on which the blood dropped.

CRIME SCENE BLOODSTAINS

Look at the bloodstains found at the crime scene. Examine the bloodstains carefully. Note that the stains are numbered. These numbers match the numbers found on the Crime Scene Sketch.

Compare the crime scene bloodstains #1–5 below to the ones found on the Bloodstain Analysis sheet. Use this data as a guide to determine the impact angle from which the blood was dropped. Write the impact angle in the second row below each stain.

	#1	#2	#3	#4	#5
Drops Found at the Crime Scene					
Degree of Impact Angle					

Carefully examine the bloodstains in the chart below. Compare the crime scene bloodstains #6–10 below to the ones found on the Bloodstain Analysis sheet. Use this data as a guide to determine the height from which each drop of blood fell to the ground. Write the answer in the column below each stain.

	#6	#7	#8	#9	#10
Drops Found at the Crime Scene					
Height From Which Blood was Dropped					

CUTS AND ABRASIONS

After analyzing the bloodstains, Detective Waldrop examined the suspects to see if any of them had a recent cut or abrasion visible to the eye that might have been responsible for the blood at the crime scene. The suspects were found to have a fresh cut, a fresh scab, a band-aid, a bandage, and a bruise. Only the bruise would not have bled. Read the following clues to determine what type of injury each suspect had and where on the body it was located.

Suspects	Scab	Bandage	Cut	Bruise	Band Aid	Left Index Finger	Right Arm	Left Elbow	Chin	Right Ankle
Theodore Newman										
Jamison Lively										
Grace St. James										
Allison Loveall										
Madison Kane										
Left Index Finger										
Right Arm										
Left Elbow										
Chin										
Right Ankle										

Clues:
1. One suspect had a bandage wrapped around her elbow.
2. Jamison had either a scab on his ankle or a bruise on his right arm.
3. Theodore cut his chin while shaving.
4. Madison and the woman with the bruise rarely injure themselves.
5. Grace had recently replaced her Band-Aid with a new one.

Can you eliminate a suspect as a result of this evidence?

_____

_____

"I COULDN'T CLIMB THAT LADDER"

After Detective Waldrop determined which suspects might be responsible for the bloodstains at the crime scene, she then considered these additional facts: Bloodstain #10 was dropped from 8 feet, indicating it had to be dropped from the ladder, and the bloody tissue was found on the platform. Detective Waldrop determined that her next goal was to see which suspect could have climbed up the ladder to the platform.

When presented with this evidence, all of the remaining suspects insisted they could not be the culprit. One claimed to have vertigo; another was fearful of heights; another afraid of ladders; and one had a knee problem. All of these conditions would have prevented the suspect from climbing up the ladder to the platform. Detective Waldrop contacted the suspects' doctors to verify their statements. She was able to reach all of them, except one—who did not have a phone number, or an address, and had not been issued a medical license. These facts indicated that a suspect might be lying.

Use the clues to solve the matrix logic puzzle to determine what condition each suspect suffers from, the doctor treating their condition, and the means by which the doctor was contacted by Detective Waldrop.

CLUES:
1. Until now, Dr. Law had not treated a patient with a fear of ladders.
2. Jamison's doctor sent a text message confirming his condition.
3. Dr. Sam phoned police to verify his patient hurt her knee last week.
4. Dr. Gice sent an e-mail about her patient with vertigo.
5. Grace St. James is afraid of heights.

Name:_____ Date:_____

"I COULDN'T CLIMB THAT LADDER"

	Fear of Heights	Knee Problem	Fear of Ladders	Vertigo	Dr. Law	Dr. Fill	Dr. Sam	Dr. Gice	E-mail	Phone	Text Message	No Phone/Address
Theodore Newman												
Jamison Lively												
Grace St. James												
Madison Kane												
E-mail												
Phone												
Text Message												
No Phone/Address												
Dr. Law												
Dr. Fill												
Dr. Sam												
Dr. Gice												

Which of these suspects might be lying, and why?

_____

_____

_____

_____

FORENSICS LAB

Become a forensic scientist and analyze stains to determine how the height from which blood is dropped affects the size of the bloodstain. Carefully follow these directions.

1. Get six index cards and label four of them with the following labels: 6 inches, one foot, 2 feet, 4 feet.

2. Now, get simulated blood (provided by your teacher), a medicine dropper, a tape measure, and a plastic garbage bag. Lay the bag down to cover the floor.

3. Lay the index card labeled 6 inches on the plastic bag. Fill the eyedropper with blood. Hold the eyedropper 6 inches directly above the card. Release four drops, one drop at a time, from the eyedropper. Move slightly to the side with each drop so the drops won't run together.

4. Next, lay the index card labeled one foot on the bag. Hold the eyedropper one foot above the card. Release four drops. Follow this procedure with the remaining two cards, using the measurements labeled on the card.

5. Now, take the extra two index cards and label them 6 feet and 8 feet. From what you have observed about the other drops, what do you think stains would look like if dropped from 6 feet? From 8 feet? Draw these stains on the cards.

FORENSICS LAB

Now analyze stains to determine how the angle from which the blood is dropped affects the shape of the stain. Carefully follow these directions:

1. Get the following supplies from your teacher: simulated blood, a medicine dropper, four angle patterns, 13 index cards, and a plastic garbage bag. Lay the bag down on the floor.

2. Get five of the index cards. These are your surface cards. Label each card: 10 degrees, 30 degrees, 50 degrees, 70 degrees, and 90 degrees.

3. Next, get the remaining index cards. Fold each one vertically in half. Using the Pattern Pieces handout, you will be cutting the index cards into angled pattern pieces. Place the pattern on one of the folded index cards, placing the "X" line on the fold. Cut out the pattern. Cut out two pieces of each pattern. Label the two pieces, using the angle degree. Then, cut out all of the remaining patterns, following these directions. These are your angled cards.

4. Place each pair of angled cards side by side on the plastic bag on the floor as directed on the pattern piece. Then, set the labeled surface cards against the matching angle cards. Lay the 10-degree surface card against the two 10-degree angled cards. Lay the 30-degree surface card against the two 30-degree angled cards. Lay the 70-degree surface card against the two 70-degree angled cards. Lay the 90-degree index card flat on the plastic sheet.

5. Fill the eyedropper with fake blood. Hold the eyedropper 6 inches above the 10-degree surface card. Release a drop of blood onto the card. Repeat this procedure on each of the labeled surface cards that are lying on their corresponding angled cards.

6. Examine the drops after you have completed all of the cards. Line them up from the smallest angle to the largest. What observations can you make about the drops? Why do you think the drops fell as they did on the impact angles?

_____

_____

_____

_____

_____

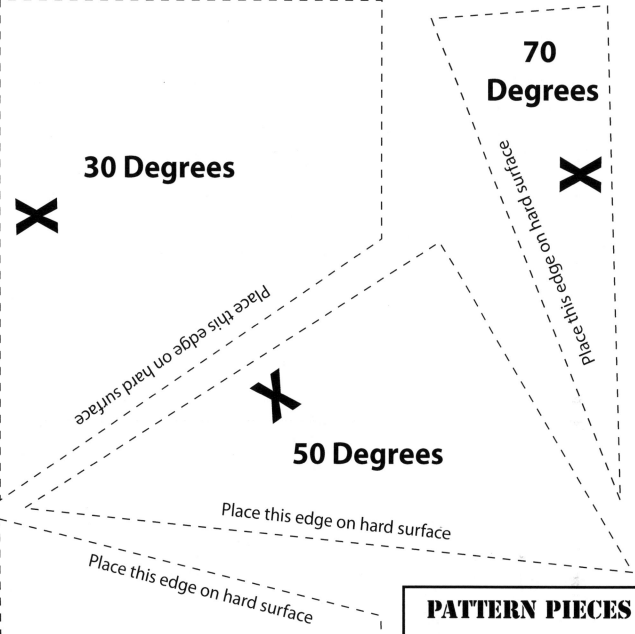

70 Degrees

Place this edge on hard surface

30 Degrees

Place this edge on hard surface

50 Degrees

Place this edge on hard surface

Place this edge on hard surface

10 Degrees

PATTERN PIECES

Directions:
1. Get eight 5" x 7" index cards and fold each one vertically in half. Cut out each pattern on an index card, placing the "X" line on the fold. Cut out two pieces of each pattern.
2. Fold the pieces and place the angled sides down on the floor as directed. Put the matching angled pieces side-by-side.
3. Lay a labeled surface card against the angle. This will be the surface on which the blood is dropped.

See the Forensics Lab handout (pp. 83–84) for detailed instructions.

DNA ANALYSIS

DNA evidence can be used to help solve crimes. DNA is found in every cell of your body. Each person's cells differ from everyone else's because everyone has different DNA. In other words, the DNA in your cells makes you unique. The only people who have the same DNA are identical twins.

Forensic scientists can compare DNA samples from two people and see that they are different. They can collect DNA from cells such as skin, blood, and other bodily fluids. After the DNA is removed from the cells, they place it in a device that separates it into its parts. These parts look much like the lines in a bar code.

Detective Waldrop examined the DNA found in the blood left at the crime scene. Then, she examined the DNA of each of the eight suspects. Can you find a match? If so, this evidence will be conclusive evidence in a court of law, proving that the suspect with the matching DNA was the person who left the blood on the stage. This person, therefore, is most likely the suspect who committed the crime.

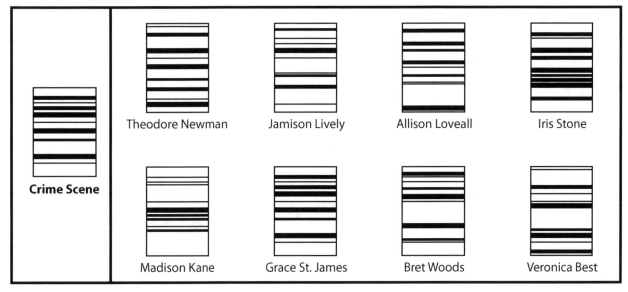

Crime Scene

Theodore Newman   Jamison Lively   Allison Loveall   Iris Stone

Madison Kane   Grace St. James   Bret Woods   Veronica Best

Which suspect has the matching DNA?_____

Review the case. Did you find other evidence that points to this suspect? Write a summary of this evidence.

_____

_____

_____

_____

_____

A VANDAL STRIKES

TEACHER'S GUIDE: A VANDAL STRIKES

Introduction

A professional football helmet is the focus of this mystery involving eight middle school students. After analyzing all of the evidence, student detectives will discover this case is a red herring—that is, things are not what they seem to be. In order to solve the case, they have to go back to square one and uncover new clues.

Preparations

In order for students to solve the mystery A Vandal Strikes, you must first prepare the crime scene evidence, Exhibits #1 and 2 (a lip print and leaves). Before your students begin solving the mystery, follow the directions in Table 1 to create these pieces of evidence.

You have the option to further challenge your students and provide a fun learning experience with the optional Forensics Lab. Setup for the Forensics Lab should take place before your students begin the activities in this mystery. The Forensics Lab includes lip print analysis that coincides with the investigation, as well as a creativity challenge in the Make Your Own Lip Print activity. Setup directions for the Forensics Lab can be found in Table 2. Note: If you choose to utilize the Forensics Lab in your classroom's crime solving, do not use the Lip Print Analysis handout (p. 97).

Solving the Mystery

Hand out A Vandal Strikes (p. 93) to introduce the mystery. Tell students that they are the detectives assigned to the case who will solve this mystery.

Discuss what happened, when it happened, and where it happened. In order to move forward with the case, the detectives will need more information. Hand out Detective Notes (p. 94). Ask students to read the statements and determine which ones are relevant to the case.

Students next will want to discuss who might have committed the crime. The logical suspects would be the students on the fundraising committee, who knew about the helmet and where it was hidden. After determining the logical suspects, students will want to then look at motive or why the suspects might have done this. Hand out The Eighth-Grade Fundraising Committee Meeting Minutes (p. 95). Have the students read this sheet and discuss if any of these students had a motive to commit this crime. Students should be able to determine that all of the students had a motive except Tom Marsalis and J. T. James.

TABLE 1
EVIDENCE SETUP

Materials
- brown, green, and dark green construction paper (one sheet each);
- one sheet of white paper;
- permanent marker;
- four plastic sandwich bags;
- scissors; and
- a pink crayon.

Instructions
1. Place the white paper over Lip Print #1 in Figure 1. Trace the pattern of the lip print onto the white paper with the pink crayon. Be sure that the pattern is clear and easy to identify.
2. Place the pink lip print in a plastic sandwich bag and label the bag Exhibit #1. Set aside.
3. Sketch Leaf #1 in Figure 1 on the brown sheet of construction paper. You may wish to photocopy and enlarge the images in Figure 1, and cut out Leaf #1 on the brown paper. Be sure to copy all of the leaf's details, like its shape, outer-edge texture, and veins.
4. Repeat Step 3 with Leaf #2 and Leaf #3 in Figure 1.
5. After you have all of your leaves copied, place them individually in plastic sandwich bags. Label all of the bags Exhibit #2. Set aside.

TABLE 2
FORENSICS LAB SETUP

Materials for the Forensics Lab
- a box of plastic sandwich bags (for evidence bags),
- a permanent marker,
- a magnifying lens,
- several sheets of white paper, and
- several different shades of red crayons and one pink crayon.

Forensics Lab Setup
1. By placing a square of white paper over Lip Print #1 in Figure 2, trace the black outline of the lip print onto the paper towel with a pink crayon. Repeat this process several more times (one evidence bag per group of 3 students), making sure that the outline is clearly visible.
2. Place the paper squares with the outline of Lip Print #1 in plastic sandwich bags, and label them Exhibit #1.
3. Repeat the tracing process for the remaining lip prints in Figure 2, Lip Prints # 2–5. Be sure to make an equal number of copies for each lip print.
4. Then place the paper squares with the remaining lip prints in sandwich bags, labeling them accordingly: Lip Print #2 = Isabel Fernandez; Lip print #3 = Ellie Johnson; Lip Print #4 = Rose Beauvoir; Lip Print #5 = Samantha Port.

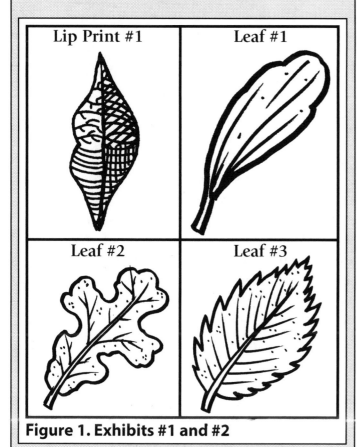

Figure 1. Exhibits #1 and #2

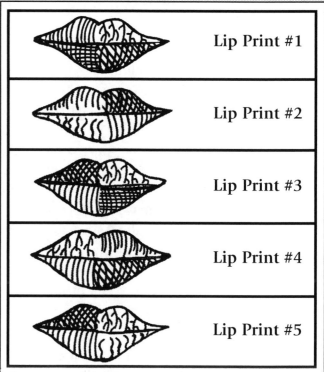

Figure 2. Lip Prints #1–5

Gathering Evidence

Hold up Exhibit #1 and Exhibit #2. Exhibit #1 consists of a tissue (or white paper) with pink lipstick found in the wastebasket next to Ms. Moondale's desk. A lip print should be easily visible on the tissue. Exhibit #2 consists of three leaves found on the floor, one beside the cabinet, one near the door to the room, and the other beneath Ms. Moondale's chair at her desk.

Lip Print Analysis

Tell students that they will analyze the lip print found on the tissue. First, discuss who might be eliminated from the suspect list because they do not wear lipstick. (Students will probably discuss that Will Wilson and Frederick Rosanelle can be eliminated because they are male, and most males do not wear lipstick.) Ask the students to consider the statements made by Ms. Moondale and the custodian when examining this evidence.

Hand out the Lip Print Classification Guide (p. 96). Read and discuss with your students, and then hand out the Lip Print Analysis sheet (p. 97) or the Lip Print Analysis Forensics Lab sheets (pp. 98–100). The Forensics Lab includes a Lip Print Analysis and Make Your Own Lip Print activity (see instructions below). After completing the Lip Print Analysis activity (with or without the lab), the students should determine that none of the girls' lip prints match the print found in Ms. Moondale's room. Discuss why this might be the case. Explain to students that they need more evidence to solve this case.

Forensics Lab Instructions

Hand out the Lip Print Analysis Forensics Lab (pp. 98–100). Instruct students to examine the suspects' lip prints (the prints that you drew in the setup). Students then need to sketch each of the suspects' prints, as well as Exhibit #1, in the data chart on p. 99. Explain that most people have different patterns on different sections of their lips. Therefore, scientists divide the lips into four sections, or quadrants. Using the Lip Print Classification Chart as a guide, instruct students to record the Roman numeral that best describes the lip print pattern in each quadrant. After examining the evidence, students should determine that none of the suspects' lip prints match Exhibit #1, the lip print found at the crime scene. As an extension to your classroom's crime solving, have students make their own lip prints (p. 100).

Leaf Analysis

Hand out the Leaf Classification Chart (p. 101). Ask students to describe all of the leaves, using the classification chart as a guide.

Students will reference this chart when observing the leaves that were collected as evidence from the crime scene.

Hand out the Leaves As Evidence sheet (p. 102). Explain to your students that they will need to analyze the leaves, but first they must gather more information in order to determine why these leaves might have been in the classroom.

Hand out Science Project (p. 103) and the crime scene evidence bags, Exhibit #2. Explain that Mr. Link's students had completed this project in class the day of the vandalism. Discuss how this information is useful. Using Exhibit #2 and the other clues student detectives have gathered so far, students should compare the suspects' leaves to the leaves found at the crime scene. Students should conclude that the culprit probably glued the leaves onto a poster for the science project and took the poster into the classroom when he or she was tampering with the helmet.

What? No Suspect?

At this point, students probably will be a little confused, after they find that none of the leaves found at the crime scene match the leaves found on the posters made by the suspects. Discuss the possible reasons for this. After discussion, ask students if this case could possibly be what's called a *red herring*. This occurs when the evidence leads down one road but after an investigation, that road is found to be a dead end. There is no evidence in this case to support the fact that one of the girls had committed the crime. Remind students there is no match not only for the leaves but for the lipstick, as well.

Detectives frequently have cases that turn out to be red herrings. Whenever this happens, they must review the evidence a second time. In this case, they must take a second look at the male suspects, even the two who appeared to have no motive. Discuss why thinking outside of the box would be helpful in reexamining the evidence.

New Evidence

Hand out Examining More Evidence (p. 104). Explain to students that they will uncover critical evidence by solving the matrix logic puzzle. After they have solved the puzzle, hand out Additional Facts (p. 105). Discuss how these facts, combined with the evidence uncovered in the logic puzzle, point to the culprit. Ask a volunteer to name the culprit and give detailed supporting evidence that proves the culprit's guilt. Then, read the Conclusion aloud to students, and congratulate them for solving the last of the *Private Eye* mysteries!

Conclusion

After this evidence was obtained, detectives confronted Will. He confessed to the crime. "I was so mad at Ellie Johnson," he said. "She's so perfect and the teacher's pet. I just wanted her to get in trouble and not me for a change. That's why I tried to frame her." Will apologized and promised to never vandalize anything again. Will's parents insisted he spend his savings on another helmet, signed by the team. Fortunately, a man at Tom's church had a cousin on the team and this was arranged. The raffle was held and was successful.

Detective Notes

Relevant Statements: Ms. Moondale: #1, 3, 5, 6, 8, 9, 11; Custodian, #1, 3, 4.

Lip Print Analysis and Forensic Lab Lip Print Analysis

Isabel Fernandez: I!, III, V, I; Ellie Johnson: III, II, I, IV; Rose Beauvoir: II, I!, I, III; Samantha Port: III, II, I, V. None of the suspects' lip prints match the crime scene evidence.

Leaves as Evidence

Leaf #1 (Red Maple)	Smooth margin Spoon-shaped Parallel veins
Leaf #2 (Post Oak)	Lobes without points Oblong Pinnate veins
Leaf #3 (American Elm)	Toothed margin Egg-shaped Pinnate veins

Science Project

Ellie Johnson's Leaves	Isabel Fernandez's Leaves
Leaf #2 (White Oak) Lobes without pointed tips Oblong Pinnate veins	Leaf #2 (American Beech) Toothed margin Elliptic shape Pinnate veins
Leaf #3 (American Chestnut) Toothed margin Lanceolate shape Pinnate veins	Leaf #3 (American Holly) Toothed margin Elliptic shape Pinnate veins

Examining More Evidence

Tom Marsalis, Mrs. Deal, So Soft, Mark Perm; J. T. James, Ms. Bell, Nose Care, Ready Mark; Frederick Rosanelle, Mr. Lee, Like Silk, Mark It; Will Wilson, Mr. Link, Dry All, Line It.

A VANDAL STRIKES

The eighth-grade class at Bellevue Middle School decided to hold a fundraiser to raise money to help build a new athletic field. Tom Marsalis, the class president, announced at a fundraising committee meeting that he would donate a professional football helmet for a raffle. Each player on the football team had signed his name in gold ink on the helmet.

"I won the helmet at a church raffle last week," Tom said. "I'm not a football fan so I'll gladly donate it for our own raffle." He said he would bring the helmet to school the next day.

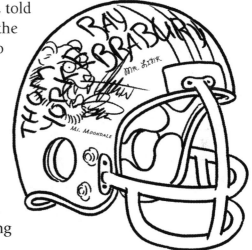

Ms. Moondale, an eighth-grade history teacher, told the committee that she would keep the helmet in the cabinet behind her desk. "I'm the only person who ever uses that cabinet," she said. "It'll be a safe place to keep the helmet until the raffle's over." Everyone agreed not to say anything about the helmet until the raffle was announced at the school's spaghetti dinner on Friday.

The next day when Tom brought the helmet to Ms. Moondale, she admired it. "Adults are going to want this helmet as much as kids will," she said. "Its value will increase over time, making it a real investment."

That day marked the end of the grading period and students got out of school at 1 p.m. Working in her room, Miss Moondale graded papers from 1 until 3 p.m., and then she went to a faculty meeting in the school cafeteria.

When the meeting ended at 4:30 p.m., Ms. Moondale headed back to her room with Mr. Link, the science teacher across the hall. "Can you keep a secret?" she asked. When he nodded, she told him about the helmet. Excited, Mr. Link insisted that she show him the prize.

Entering her room, Ms. Moondale noticed the door to the cabinet. It was wide open. "That's odd," she said. "I know I closed that cabinet door." She glanced up at the third shelf. The football helmet was sitting just where she had left it. "Thank goodness," she said. "I thought for a minute that something was wrong."

Mr. Link reached for the helmet and examined it closely. "I'm afraid something is," he said. "I don't think you're a member of this team." He put the helmet down on the desk and pointed to Ms. Moondale's name. It was printed in gold letters below the signature of the team's star quarterback.

Ms. Moondale frowned. "And, neither are you," she said. She drew her finger across the helmet to Mr. Link's name printed right next to the team's coach.

The two teachers searched the helmet and were dismayed to find the principal's name printed near Mr. Link's and the assistant principal's name printed just above it. "No one will want the helmet now," Ms. Moondale said. "I'm afraid our fundraiser is ruined."

DETECTIVE NOTES

When questioned by detectives, Ms. Moondale and the custodian made the following statements. Put a check mark beside the statements that are relevant to the case.

Ms. Moondale's Statements:

_____ 1. "My classroom is on the second floor in the eighth-grade wing."

_____ 2. "My classroom is the largest one on the second floor."

_____ 3. "The school cafeteria is on the first floor across from the office in the sixth-grade wing."

_____ 4. "The school cafeteria is the only place that is large enough for the whole faculty to meet together in a meeting."

_____ 5. "I never lock the door to my classroom when I go to a faculty meeting."

_____ 6. "The custodian cleaned my room around 2:30 p.m. while I was grading papers at my desk."

_____ 7. "I always grade papers sitting at my desk."

_____ 8. "I never mentioned the helmet to the custodian or to anyone other than Mr. Link."

_____ 9. "As usual, the custodian emptied my trashcan that afternoon. When I left the room to go to the faculty meeting, I just happened to glance down at the can. It was empty."

_____ 10. "The trashcan in my room is always full at the end of the day."

_____ 11. "No one else came into my room after the custodian left."

The Custodian's Statements:

_____ 1. "I finished cleaning all of the rooms on the second floor around 3:30 p.m."

_____ 2. "It takes me about 20 minutes to clean each room."

_____ 3. "I didn't see anyone in the hall after 3 p.m. when all of the teachers went down to the faculty meeting."

_____ 4. "After I finished on the second floor, I went to clean the sixth-grade wing."

_____ 5. "I have been the custodian in this building for 12 years."

THE EIGHTH-GRADE FUNDRAISING COMMITTEE MEETING MINUTES

January 14, Ms. Moondale's Room
Committee Members Present: Tom Marsalis, Chairman; Rose Beauvoir; Isabel Fernandez; J. T. James; Ellie Johnson; Samantha Port; Frederick Rosanelle; Will Wilson; Ms. Moondale, Sponsor

Tom Marsalis called the meeting to order. He reported that he would donate a football helmet, signed by team members of a professional football team, to the school for a raffle to earn money for the new athletic field.

Discussion followed. Frederick Rosanelle didn't like the idea of the raffle. He stated that he thought the school would make more money if they had a dance and sold tickets to it. He volunteered his rock band, Hot Dog, to play at the dance at no cost.

Isabel Fernandez agreed with Rosanelle. She stated that the band is popular and students would love a dance. She is the lead singer in the band. She insisted that kids would like dancing to their band better than owning a football helmet.

J. T. James disagreed. He thought the raffle for a helmet was a great idea and he stated that he would buy at least 20 tickets himself in the hope of winning it.

Will Wilson suggested raffling off a soccer ball instead. He said that he was sick of football and stated that soccer is a much better sport.

Ellie Johnson expressed concern that no one was considering other things that were needed at the school. She argued that money should be raised for new band uniforms rather than for the athletic field. She pointed out that the school board had already designated money for the football field.

Will disputed this, stating that the school board had never had money in the school's budget for a new athletic field. He stated that Ellie always acted like she knew everything when she didn't and he asked that her statement be struck from the minutes because it wasn't true. Ellie argued that it was. Ms. Moondale interceded and stated that the claim was legitimate.

Samantha Port agreed with Ellie and stated that too much money was already being spent on sports but never for the arts. She suggested having a raffle to support the school's theatre group by selling tickets to the school's upcoming musical. She asked why anyone would want to buy an old helmet that is dirty and smelly.

Rose Beauvoir claimed that the band needed the money more than the theatre group. She plays the clarinet in the band and described the uniforms as old and ratty. She stated that it wasn't fair that football always got all of the attention.

Ms. Moondale stated that because Tom had freely donated the helmet, the committee should support the raffle. She said that she was sorry the committee didn't all agree but as sponsor, she would make the final decision, and her decision was to raffle off the helmet. Ms. Moondale said that she would keep the helmet in her room in the cabinet behind her desk. The committee agreed not to say anything about the helmet until the raffle was announced at the school's spaghetti dinner to be held on Friday.

Tom Marsalis moved to adjourn the meeting, Rose seconded the motion. The motion passed, and the meeting was adjourned.

LIP PRINT CLASSIFICATION GUIDE

Detectives found a piece of tissue in the trashcan in Ms. Moondale's classroom. The tissue had a lip print on it. You need to analyze the lip print based on the characteristics discussed in this classification guide. Your teacher will display this evidence to you as Exhibit #1.

Every individual in the world is unique. Lip prints, like fingerprints, illustrate this uniqueness because no two lip prints are alike. The study of lip prints is called *cheiloscopy*.

The prints are formed by tiny wrinkles and grooves on the surface of the lips. These grooves form a variety of patterns. Forensic scientists can analyze the pattern of a lip print found at a crime scene and use it to identify the person who left the print.

Lip Print Pattern Classification Guide

Type I: Long Vertical Grooves	Type I!: Short Vertical Grooves	Type II: Branched Grooves
Type III: Intersected Grooves	Type IV: Rectangular Grooves	Type V: Irregular Grooves

Note that Type I and Type I! are both vertical grooves and therefore have the same Roman numeral. The "!" differentiates the short from the long pattern.

LIP PRINT ANALYSIS

Most people have different groove patterns on different parts of their lips. For this reason, forensic scientists divide the lips into four sections, or quadrants, when they examine a lip print.

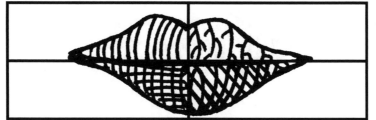

Left Upper Quadrant   Right Upper Quadrant

Left Lower Quadrant   Right Lower Quadrant

Note that this diagram is reversed, making a mirror image. When looking at a suspect face to face, you are seeing his left side as your right. The diagrams are always reversed for this reason.

Examine the sketch of the lip print found at the crime scene in Ms. Moondale's room, Exhibit #1 (shown above). Use a pencil and mark the four quadrants on the sketches of the suspects' lip prints. Using the Lip Print Classification Chart as a guide, determine what type of pattern is in each quadrant of their lip prints. Write the Roman numeral that names that type of pattern in the appropriate box. See the example on the chart below.

Lip Prints	Lip Print Sketch	Left Upper Quadrant	Right Upper Quadrant	Left Lower Quadrant	Right Lower Quadrant
Exhibit #1 (Ms. Moondale's room)		I	II	IV	III
Isabel Fernandez					
Ellie Johnson					
Rose Beauvoir					
Samantha Port					

Does one of the suspect's prints match the above print found in Ms. Moondale's room?

_____

LIP PRINT ANALYSIS FORENSICS LAB

Most people have different groove patterns on different parts of their lips. For this reason, forensic scientists divide the lips into four sections, or quadrants, when they examine the lip print.

Left Upper Quadrant 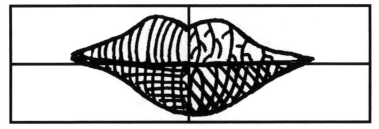 Right Upper Quadrant

Left Lower Quadrant   Right Lower Quadrant

Note that this diagram is reversed, making a mirror image. When looking at a suspect face to face, you are seeing his left side as your right. The diagrams are always reversed for this reason.

Follow the steps below to analyze the lip print found in Ms. Moondale's room and the lip prints made by each of the remaining suspects. Compare the prints to determine if there is a match.

1. Get Exhibit #1. Lay the print flat on your desk. Look at the left upper quadrant. Remember, this is to your left. What is the pattern? Record on the data sheet the Roman numeral that best describes the pattern in this quadrant. Use the Lip Print Pattern Classification Chart as a guide. Now, examine each of the other quadrants and record your data.

2. Next, examine each of the suspect's prints and record in your data chart.

3. Sketch the lip print in the chart and then record "yes" if the sketch is a match to the evidence or "no" if it is not.

LIP PRINT ANALYSIS FORENSICS LAB

Lip Prints	Lip Print Sketch	Left Upper Quadrant	Right Upper Quadrant	Left Lower Quadrant	Right Lower Quadrant
Exhibit #1 (Ms. Moondale's room)					
Isabel Fernandez					
Ellie Johnson					
Rose Beauvoir					
Samantha Port					

Does one of the suspect's prints match the print found in Ms. Moondale's room?

_____

MAKE YOUR OWN LIP PRINT

Draw a sketch of your completed lip print.

Left Upper Quadrant	Right Upper Quadrant
Left Lower Quadrant	Right Lower Quadrant

Analyze your lip prints to determine what patterns you find on your own lips. Gather the following materials for this activity from your instructor:

- lip balm or lipstick,
- cotton swabs,
- an index card,
- dusting powder (chocolate cocoa),
- dusting brush,
- paper towel,
- magnifying lens, and
- Lip Print Classification Guide (p. 96).

Follow these steps to analyze your own print:

1. Put lip balm or lipstick on your lips, using a cotton swab.
2. Fold the index card and press your lips on the card at the fold.
3. Unfold the card and write your name below your print.
4. Put the card on a paper towel and dust with the dusting powder. Do not put too much powder on the print.
5. Shake the powder off of the card.
6. Examine the print closely, using a magnifying lens. What type of pattern do you see? Examine each quadrant closely.
7. Then sketch your lip print and match the quadrant patterns to the characteristics listed in the Lip Classification Guide.

LEAF CLASSIFICATION CHART

MARGINS (Leaf's edges)	SHAPE (Overall shape)			VENNATION (Vein arrangement)
Smooth	**Long**	**Elliptic** (Wide in the center, narrowing at each tip)	**Kidney-shaped**	**Pinnate Veins** Arranged with one large vein in the center and smaller veins branching off of it.
Toothed Jagged edge	**Lanceolate** (Shaped like a lance with a pointed tip)	**Egg-shaped**	**Spoon-shaped**	**Palmate Veins** Arranged with two or more large veins fanning out from the base of the leaf.
Lobed **With Pointed Tips**	**Oblong** (Long and wide)	**Heart-shaped**	**Round**	**Parallel Veins** Veins run parallel to one another.
Lobed **Without Pointed Tips**				**Netted Veins** Veins connect like in a net.

LEAVES AS EVIDENCE

Three leaves were found in Ms. Moondale's room after the vandalism (Exhibit #2). The bottom side of each leaf was covered with a sticky substance determined by forensic experts to be glue. Examine each leaf in its evidence bag and write its description, using the Leaf Classification Chart as a guide.

Leaf #1	Description 2–4 in. long
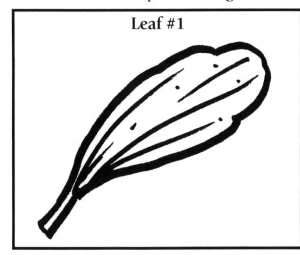	

Leaf #2	Description 6–10 in. long
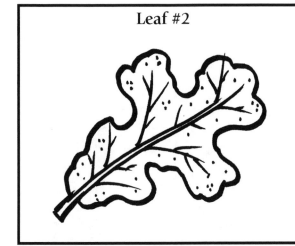	

Leaf #3	Description 3–5 in. long
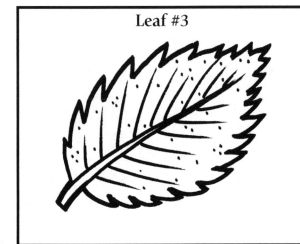	

Name:_____ Date:_____

SCIENCE PROJECT

Students in Mr. Link's science class completed a project while studying trees. They each made a poster, identifying two types of leaves found in their backyards. Mr. Link told detectives the names of the trees researched by the suspects.

Examine each leaf and write its description, using the Leaf Classification Chart as a guide and the first two leaves as an example. The length of each leaf has been provided.

Compare the leaves the suspects used on their poster with the leaves found in Ms. Moondale's classroom. Do any of the leaves match the ones found at the crime scene?

Ellie Johnson's Leaves	Description	Isabel Fernandez's Leaves	Description
Silver Maple	• 2 ½–5 in. long • Lobed with pointed tips • Heart-shaped • Palmate veins	Scarlet Oak	• 3–7 in. long • Lobed with pointed tips • Oblong shaped • Pinnate veins
White Oak	• 4–7 in. long	American Beech	• 2 ½–5 ½ in. long
American Chestnut	• 5–8 in. long	American Holly	• 2–4 in. long

EXAMINING MORE EVIDENCE

Detectives gathered more information in their reinvestigation of the four male suspects. The boys each had a different science teacher and used a different brand of tissue. They each had a set of permanent ink markers in their desk; however, each set was a different brand.

Read the clues to determine the name of each teacher, the type of tissue, and the brand of permanent marker that each student used.

	Mr. Link	Ms. Bell	Mrs. Deal	Mr. Lee	So Soft	Like Silk	Dry All	Nose Care	Ready Mark	Mark It	Mark Perm	Line It
Tom Marsalis												
J. T. James												
Frederick Rosanelle												
Will Wilson												
Ready Mark												
Mark It												
Mark Perm												
Line It												
So Soft												
Like Silk												
Dry All												
Nose Care												

Clues:

1. Frederick had a box of Like Silk tissue in his desk in Mr. Lee's room.
2. The suspect in Ms. Bell's room used Nose Care tissues and Ready Mark markers.
3. Tom uses So Soft tissues.
4. Will likes Dry All tissues and Line It markers but was not in Mrs. Deal's room.
5. Tom does not like Mark It markers.

ADDITIONAL FACTS

After you have solved the puzzle,
examine these additional facts.

- Only Mr. Link had assigned the
  leaf project to his students.
- Mr. Link handed the project back
  to Will the day of the crime for
  him to take home.
- Three leaves were missing from
  Will's poster. The types of leaves
  that were missing were the same
  type of leaves found in Ms.
  Moondale's classroom.
- The tissue found in the trashcan
  in Ms. Moondale's room was
  analyzed at the forensics lab and was found to be the Dry All brand.
- The ink analysis indicated the culprit had used a Line It marker to
  write the names on the helmet.
- A loose tissue was found on the floor of Will's locker. The tissue was
  smeared with lipstick. It was the same shade and brand as that found
  in the trashcan.
- Mr. Link said that Ellie Johnson, Will's lab partner complained that
  Will played around most of the time and she ended up having to do
  all of the work. Mr. Link had told Will that because he had not done
  his share in the lab, he was going to get a D on his report card.

Considering all of these facts and the evidence indicated in the puzzle, are
you able to identify the culprit? Identify him or her, and list several reasons
why you believe this is the culprit.

_____

_____

_____

_____

_____

_____

THE MYSTERY
LEARNING CENTER

TEACHER'S GUIDE:
THE MYSTERY LEARNING CENTER

Introduction

Learning centers are a valuable tool for teachers when differentiating instruction. A mystery center can be used to challenge students to reach beyond what they have learned in this workbook and apply the learned skills to activities such as writing their own mystery, drawing a crime scene, and creating their own logic puzzles to help others solve their crime.

Setting Up the Learning Center

Make copies of Write Your Own Mystery, Sketch Your Crime Scene, and Write Your Own Logic Puzzles (pp. 108–111) to use in the learning center. Provide paper and colored pencils for students to use.

Encourage students to read and solve the mysteries written by their classmates. You may wish to hold onto their written mysteries and accompanying handouts for later use, (e.g., in the next mystery day that you have in your classroom). This will motivate and excite your students to do a good job thinking through their own mysteries as they go through the planning and writing process.

WRITE YOUR OWN MYSTERY

This is your chance to be creative and write a mystery using your own imagination. Try to make your mystery different from the ones you have been working on in your classroom.

The following steps will help you plan out the details of your mystery. After you've mapped out the clues of your mystery, it's up to you to write a story tying all of your clues together. Choose the information you include in your story very carefully—remember, this is a mystery! Include a paragraph that describes the solution of your mystery.

On a blank sheet of notebook paper, begin planning your mystery using the steps below.

1. Choose a *setting* where the mystery takes place, such as a castle, library, museum, school, archaeological dig, or a soda pop factory.
2. Choose a *crime* that will take place in the setting, such as a catnapping, a hoax, a blackmail, a robbery, or a forgery.
3. Create a *scenario* in which the crime is committed, such as opening night at the amusement park, a new discovery at an archaeological dig, a new recipe for a soda pop is soon to be announced, and so on.
4. Describe the *victim*. Remember the different tools that were used in the mysteries you have been solving in your classroom, such as newspaper clippings or character's descriptions of the victim. Tools like these can be used to describe the victim in your mystery.
5. Choose a *culprit*. Describe the culprit. Give details about his or her life. Then, answer these questions about the culprit. Why would he or she commit the crime? When could he or she commit the crime? How would he or she commit the crime?
6. Choose two other *suspects*. Write a brief description of each one. Write a motive for one suspect. Write why the other suspect would have no motive or reason to commit the crime.
7. Choose one clue that points to the culprit but not to the other suspects. Describe the clue.
8. Write a short outline of how the crime will occur.

Now you're ready to piece together all of your clues into your own mystery! Write a mystery for your classmates to solve. You may refer to the other mysteries that you solved in *The Private Eye School* as examples of length and details.

SKETCH YOUR CRIME SCENE

This is another opportunity for you to use the knowledge of crime scene investigation that you have learned to create a drawing of your own imaginary crime scene. You were asked to write your own mystery—now, draw a picture of the crime scene in your mystery. Use your answers to the handout Write Your Own Mystery to recall the details of the setting and characters in your mystery.

Ask yourself these questions: What happened? What clues were left behind at the scene?

Here are some examples of trace evidence. Use these examples to help create a scene of your mystery.

Possible trace evidence:
- hair,
- thread,
- footprint,
- lip print,
- fingerprint,
- tire print,
- tool impression,
- dust particles, and
- pieces of a leaf.

Other evidence that might be found at the scene:
- glass fragment,
- mystery powder,
- ransom note,
- torn ticket,
- candy wrapper, and
- store receipt.

After you have sketched your mystery's crime scene, use colored pencils to add color to your drawing—this will make your drawing look similar to a photograph that an investigator would take to help solve the crime.

WRITE YOUR OWN LOGIC PUZZLES

Write a logic puzzle that pertains to the mystery you wrote. Put the three suspects from your mystery in the puzzle. For a challenge, make up two more suspects to use in the puzzle. Then, follow these steps and write the puzzle.

1. Write the names of five suspects in the first column in the chart below.
2. Choose an attribute to describe the suspects and write each attribute in the top row in the chart (e.g., if you chose facial marks, write "No Marks, Scar, Mole, Wart, and Pimples" in the top row.) Next, decide which suspect has a particular attribute. List the suspects and the attributes on another sheet of paper. This is your answer key.
3. Write the clues for your puzzle. Then, ask a friend to solve your puzzle.

WRITE YOUR OWN LOGIC PUZZLES

Clues:

1. _____

_____

_____

2. _____

_____

_____

3. _____

_____

_____

4. _____

_____

_____

5. _____

_____

_____

After you complete your mystery's logic puzzle, you may want to consider creating a second, or third puzzle to give detectives more clues about your mystery. When you have completed your mystery, trade it with classmates. Happy sleuthing!

ABOUT THE AUTHOR

Mary Ann Carr, a 30-year veteran educator, began writing mysteries for kids to solve while teaching gifted students in Hanover County, VA. Her current projects include a parent's toolkit, designed to help parents complement the education offered by schools, and a series of CSI-like mysteries to help children develop critical thinking and deductive reasoning skills while solving crimes.

Mary Ann holds a master's degree in curriculum development from Virginia Commonwealth University. She and her husband live on a small harbor off the Chesapeake Bay in Mathews County, VA.

COMMON CORE STATE STANDARDS ALIGNMENT

Grade Level	Common Core State Standards in ELA-Literacy
Grade 4	RF.4.3 Know and apply grade-level phonics and word analysis skills in decoding words
	RF.4.4 Read with sufficient accuracy and fluency to support comprehension.
Grade 5	RF.5.3 Know and apply grade-level phonics and word analysis skills in decoding words.
	RF.5.4 Read with sufficient accuracy and fluency to support comprehension.
Grade 6	RI.6.1 Cite textual evidence to support analysis of what the text says explicitly as well as inferences drawn from the text.

Printed in the United States
by Baker & Taylor Publisher Services